T0208865

Life's Callings

Guidance for a Fulfilling Journey

JOE C. BROWN

WESTBOW
PRESS®
A DIVISION OF THOMAS NELSON
& ZONDERVAN

This book is a work of non-fiction. Unless otherwise noted, the author and the publisher make no explicit guarantees as to the accuracy of the information contained in this book and in some cases, names of people and places have been altered to protect their privacy.

WestBow Press books may be ordered through booksellers or by contacting:

WestBow Press
A Division of Thomas Nelson & Zondervan
1663 Liberty Drive
Bloomington, IN 47403
www.westbowpress.com
844-714-3454

Because of the dynamic nature of the Internet, any web addresses or links contained in this book may have changed since publication and may no longer be valid. The views expressed in this work are solely those of the author and do not necessarily reflect the views of the publisher, and the publisher hereby disclaims any responsibility for them.

Any people depicted in stock imagery provided by Getty Images are models, and such images are being used for illustrative purposes only.
Certain stock imagery © Getty Images.

ISBN: 978-1-6642-7113-5 (sc)
ISBN: 978-1-6642-7114-2 (hc)
ISBN: 978-1-6642-7112-8 (e)

Library of Congress Control Number: 2022912166

Print information available on the last page.

WestBow Press rev. date: 09/15/2022

Contents

Acknowledgments ix

Preface xi

Part I—The Four Dimensions of Life's Callings

Chapter 1   Life's Callings 1
Chapter 2   The Gospel Call 19
Chapter 3   The Vocational Call...................................... 33
Chapter 4   Our Christian Calling.................................. 53
Chapter 5   The Special Call 71

Part II—Guidance for a Fulfilling Journey

Chapter 6   God: The Caller of the Called 93
Chapter 7   How God Speaks 111
Chapter 8   Seeking Divine Guidance 129
Chapter 9   God's Anointed..147
Chapter 10   Has God Called You?...................................165

Bibliography...183

Acknowledgments

I want to thank the thousands of students across three decades who have taught me so much about life's callings. As is true of the teaching-learning process, I have learned from my students much about how God speaks, calling us into the paths of eternal life and His will for our lives. They have brought a multitude of questions to the classroom, and some of those questions have taken considerable time to find suitable answers that satisfy their quest for truth.

The classroom has provided a goldmine of resources for learning how the Lord moves to call people into His service and how He works in concert with church leaders in raising new understudies who will lead the church in the future.

Writing this book has been a long and tedious process that I thought would go much quicker than it did. Initially, I expected it to take a couple of years, but it has taken more than a decade from its initial stages to completion of the manuscript. In the process, I have learned a lot. My understanding of how the Lord works calling people into His service has broadened significantly. I also came to understand how even now the Lord is at work in the hearts and minds of a new generation of believers, birthing within them innovative ways to do ministry. While it may take the established church some time to catch up with how the Lord is at work calling His servants into the whitened harvest fields, the one who oversees the course of history never ceases to work building His kingdom.

Thank you to Anita Conkel, Korrin Miller Richey, and Amber Ginter, for your help in the editing process. Anita was a colleague who helped me with a lot of the editing. Korrin and Amber, former students, carefully read the text, adding editorial notes, questions, and notes of affirmations that encouraged me in the writing process. Their notes provoked new insights that contributed significantly to improving the book.

I would also be remiss if I did not give tremendous credit to my family. They knew Dad was at work on a book that seemingly was taking forever to complete. At times, they questioned if it would ever be completed. However, they were always there to encourage me to finish the project.

Finally, thanks to my wife, Carol, who has patiently borne with me through this whole process. When I was dedicating much of my summer breaks to writing, revising, and editing the work, she was patient with me. She, too, has taught me much about how to communicate with others. She writes so easily and beautifully, while for me it is a laborious process to get my words written in a manner that expresses what I am thinking. She has been my inspiration in life for these past fifty-eight years.

Preface

Most of my career has been spent working in institutions of higher learning that were founded to prepare ministers for ministry. Although some of these institutions have expanded their missions, at their core, the focus remains to educate students who have a calling to serve in ministry. As a result, many of the students who enroll in these institutions arrive at college with the question on some level, "Should I become a minister?"

Part of the time while I was writing this book, it was my privilege to work on the staff of one of the fastest-growing churches in my denomination. A key factor that attracted me to the church was how the lead pastor was recruiting young people for ministry. He not only recruited them but also promoted these young men and women as they launched their careers. It appeared there was a connection between his vision for getting people into the ministry and the remarkable growth of his church.

This seed idea for this book came following an interview with a middle-aged man in the early 1990s who stopped by my office to inquire if we had any programs that would prepare him for the ministry, where he did not need to uproot his family and move to our campus. At that time, distance education and adult higher education were in their formative stages, and I didn't have a suitable answer for him. However, I could not get his dilemma out of my mind.

A few years later, I ended up working in an innovative program that trained second-career adults for ministry. I began interviewing students about their call to ministry which initiated my research into how the Lord calls people into the ministry.

Later, while serving as a vice president of a university, for several years I taught a senior capstone class for ministry students. In that course, I had my students write about what they felt their calling in life was. From their papers, I drafted a couple dozen questions that kept reappearing as they wrote about their callings. That list provided the outline for this book.

This book does not answer every question that may arise as a person seeks to answer whether the Lord is calling them into the ministry. Rather, it examines the broad spectrum of all that is involved in the call of God, especially the call to ministry. An early part of the book describes how the words *call* and *calling* and associated words are used in the scriptures and provide the foundation for the outline of the book.

The book aims to encourage young people to give serious consideration to a career in ministry. They are challenged to take seriously Jesus's challenge to pray for "the Lord of the harvest … to send out workers into his harvest field" (Matthew 9:38 NIV). It is not unusual that when people begin to pray about this need for Christian workers, the Lord begins to speak to them, calling them into the fields of His work.

It is my prayer that this book will help those who are seeking direction for their careers, especially a career in ministry, to gain a broadened understanding of how God calls people into His service.

PART I

The Four Dimensions of Life's Callings

Life's Callings

> The harvest is plentiful but the workers are few. Ask the Lord of the harvest, therefore, to send out workers into his harvest field.
>
> —Matthew 9:37–38 (NIV)

Introduction

For the past decade, I have taught a capstone course for university ministry students. In that course, I ask students to describe what they believe to be their calling in life. It is interesting to read their papers and then observe as their aspirations and dreams take shape when they launch their careers.

This process has enabled me to identify many of the questions students have about their future—especially as it relates to the calling to ministry.

Confusion arises when they hear some preachers teach that every Christian is called to ministry and hear other preachers preach that God only calls some people to the ministry. They hear stories about how outstanding Christian leaders were specifically called to their work by the Lord and ask if that is the way it works for everyone. Another group of students asks if calling is not just recognizing a need in our world and seeking to do something about it. They ask if this inner voice is enough evidence to be understood as a calling to ministry. The truth lies within both experiences.

While the call to ministry is straightforward, describing it can become more complex and tedious. Some of this complexity lies in the fact that the Lord often uses multiple ways to call people into the ministry. Throughout church history, these methods have varied and been shaped to some extent by the culture and its times.

In some cases, the call is simple, straightforward, and dramatic. It is so clear there is little room for doubt. In other cases, the call may take some time, an event, or a sequence of events. Attempting to describe all these methods and reduce them to a few basic, understandable principles is challenging.

To begin the discussion, these questions are posed: What do you believe to be your calling in life? What captures your attention, stirs your passions, and helps you focus on a purpose for your life? What are you skilled at doing? What do you find interesting to the point that you keep circling back to it? A calling often involves all these factors and sometimes is not a single event or experience. It is a series of events and experiences that launch a career in ministry.

While the seed idea of the calling may start with a single event or idea, over time, it takes deeper root in our minds and thoughts; we keep coming back to it, giving it more consideration each time. While it may begin with a simple inner urge to do something about a particular need in our world, it often grows from that seed thought to become a strong inner drive to serve that need in the church and society.

The idea of calling is associated with the word *service* and is what motivates us to serve our world. In a religious setting, the words *service* and *ministry* are used interchangeably. In fact, in the New Testament, the words translated *service* and *ministry* come from the same Greek word.

Our initial impressions about serving in ministry often arise from seemingly random experiences in life. As these thoughts continue to occur in our minds, questions arise about what we should do about them. Over time, the idea grows into a conviction that we ought to do something about a need in our world or the church. This conviction eventually becomes the guiding force in life that shapes our careers.

While calling is often discussed in simple terms, it is not as easy to describe as it may seem. In the journey of life, we discover there are many voices vying for our attention as we forge our careers. At times, it seems we are being pulled in several directions at the same time, and sometimes, they appear to be opposing each other. What are we to do when we find ourselves in this situation?

Our goal in this book is not to develop a series of steps to follow to determine our calling in life. Rather, it is to examine the broader range of life's callings and see how they are related to the call to ministry. The key idea is to discover how all these bear upon the call to ministry.

The first five chapters explore the broad spectrum of life's callings in general and touch on virtually all aspects of life that are related to a career. Chapters 6 through 9 focus on how God speaks to us when He calls us and how to recognize His voice. The final chapter deals with the responsibility we are entrusted with to answer the Lord's call.

In this book, the *special call* of God is defined as what a person experiences when God calls them to dedicate their lives to ministry as a vocation. *Miriam-Webster's Dictionary* defines a *special call* as a "strong urge toward a particular way of life, career, or vocation (Webster 1996)." It is the inner conviction about our purpose for being on this earth.

At times, it is associated with the circumstances of our life and takes into consideration the spiritual, physical, and material needs of the people around us, causing us to recognize and embrace a sense of responsibility to serve those needs. Most denominations consider the *special call* of God a requisite for ordination. Ordination boards attempt to carefully vet those who seek ordination to determine if indeed they have been called by the Lord.

A special calling is not something that a person casually experiments with to determine whether they should become a minister. Rather, it is the recognition of God's voice calling them to His work and motivating them to seek the church's affirmation through its ordination process.

Vocational Ministry

When *vocational ministry* is mentioned, a lot of questions arise. Some think about the current need for pastors, especially for smaller congregations. The current trends indicate that many are leaving after about ten years in ministry. Others think about the current increase in the number of women entering the ministry. Others think about the recent developments of house churches or the trend of megachurches that are often started separately from denominational sponsorship. In light of these trends, there is the concern about if there will be enough ministers to serve the church. During His ministry, Jesus proclaimed, "The harvest is plentiful but the workers are few" (Matthew 9:37 NIV). During these times, there are not enough workers for the harvest.

I recently asked one of my students where he attended church. He shared that he originally relocated to the area to plant a church. When he started the church plant, he expected it to grow to a congregation of a thousand. However, that did not happen. Six months after their launch, the gatherings had grown to about thirty people. However, after a couple of years, the group had dwindled to fewer than a dozen. He indicated that most of the three or four families that were a part of the gatherings were also attending established churches.

When I inquired about his major, he shared that he had started as a ministry major then switched to teacher education. The prospect of having a church of the size that could support him and his family had faded, and he was now pursuing what he perceived to be a viable profession to support his family and allow for ministry. The question that came to mind was this: what exactly was the Lord calling him to do?

One of the key questions raised when discussing the call to ministry is this: how do we hear the *special call* to ministry? On the surface, the answer appears to be simple: God is the one who calls people into the ministry. However, as we probe deeper into the question, several other factors arise. Why aren't more people being called into the ministry? The need for ministers is now greater than it has ever been in my lifetime. Are people not hearing the call, or are they ignoring or rejecting the call? Why are so many ministers leaving the ministry? Is it because they are no longer called? Have they fallen away from Christ? Is it because the church is in spiritual decline, and they have been swept up in this spiritual decline? Or perhaps some have misunderstood their calling and feel they are not suited for ministry? Why is the need for ministers trending upward while the number of those preparing to enter ministry is trending downward?

If we limit our discussion to God's role in calling people to ministry, we may overlook a significant part of that responsibility. Does the church have any responsibility in the calling of people to the ministry? Do ministers and church leaders have any responsibility in calling talented young men and women into the ministry? On his second missionary journey, after choosing Silas as a coworker for his mission, when Paul came to Lystra, he chose Timothy as his apprentice and took him along as an understudy.

Later, Timothy was put in charge of the church in Ephesus. It is a mistake to conclude that this was solely the voice of God speaking to Timothy, without Paul's actions. Paul recognized Timothy's potential for ministry and selected him as an understudy. Certainly, Paul sought the Lord's help and was under the leadership of the Spirit when he added Timothy to his team. While in the ultimate sense, it was God's voice that Timothy heard about his career choice, it was Paul and the elders in Lystra who physically laid their hands on Timothy, commissioning him to the ministry. (See Acts 16.) Is the church missing something today?

Life is complex, with many voices vying for our attention about serving the needs in our world. Many of these are legitimate. How do we recognize and heed the voice of God—especially when it comes to the special call to ministry?

To answer this question, several areas of life's callings are examined to gain a good overview of how these concerns and responsibilities are interrelated and connected to God's calling. There is usually a certain amount of tension involved in most career decisions, especially in the initial stages. To describe this process, life's callings are divided into four basic categories. Each category is briefly defined considering its area of responsibility. The goal is to keep all these areas of responsibility in balance as we forge our career paths, particularly the call to ministry. The end goal is to help the reader answer the question, "Is the Lord calling me into the ministry?"

The special call to ministry is discussed in the context of life's other callings. It is like unscrambling a Rubik's Cube after it has been scrambled. A Rubik's Cube has six faces, and initially, each face has a uniform color. However, with just a few twists of each side, all the colors are quickly scrambled. The goal then is to realign the pieces so that once again all the faces have a uniform color. Examining life's callings is a lot like attempting to unscramble a scrambled Rubik's Cube. Life comes to us somewhat like a scrambled Rubik's Cube; our job is to unscramble it.

Another analogy that can be used to describe life's callings is to compare them to vector forces that pull us in several different directions at once. Determining our calling is like a pilot navigating an airplane from point A to point B with crosswinds blowing. As the plane moves along its path, crosswinds are continually changing the plane's speed and direction as it charts a trajectory to its destination. Each shift of the wind's direction or velocity alters the plane's speed and path. The pilot must navigate through all these vector forces to safely reach the right destination. In a sense, the trajectory of a career in ministry can be compared to this process.

A third analogy is to think of life's callings like the strands of a rope. Each strand represents a particular area of responsibility in life that vies for our attention; they are calling us to take responsibility for all areas of our lives. Just as the strands of a rope are intertwined to form a single cord, similarly, our life is a single path of combined responsibilities that shape the trajectory of our career.

The Four Categories of Life's Calling

For our discussion, life's callings are divided into four primary categories. Each category represents a particular strand of the rope, or color on each face of the Rubik's Cube, or a specific vector force in our lives. They include our *vocational calling*, the *gospel call*, our *Christian calling*, and the *special call* to ministry. All these callings are discussed in the scriptures and use the words *call* and *calling*. They are briefly described below and developed more in depth in subsequent chapters.

Vocational Calling

The first category of life's callings is our *vocational calling*. This calling was given to Adam in the Garden of Eden and subsequently to every member of humanity. In the very first chapter of the Bible, God called Adam to take care of the earth and rule over it. It involved cultivating the soil, populating the earth, ruling over the animal kingdom, and seeking to make the earth and its environment a better place in which to live and work. This command was given while the first pair were living in paradise and before sin entered the world. The expression *one's calling in life* is often used to refer to this calling and is used to describe a person's line of work and vocational tasks in life. It is used in this manner in both religious settings as well as in secular circles. It describes the inner motivation a person has to pursue a particular vocation and assumes the person has the skills and intellect necessary to perform their work.

The Gospel Calling

The second category of life's callings is the *gospel call* or the call to salvation. This describes God's invitation prompting us to look to Him and trust Him for our salvation. It is what Jesus meant when He said, "I have not come to call the righteous, but sinners to repentance" (Luke 5:32 NIV).

The first hint of this call was given to Adam and Eve while they were in the Garden of Eden, after they sinned. The Bible describes this event as a time when the Lord God came walking through the garden in the cool of the day to meet with Adam, as He did every day. However, on the day after Adam sinned, He called to the man, "Adam where are you?" (Genesis 3:9 NIV). Something had happened that altered Adam's relationship with his Creator. It was the initial foreshadowing of the *gospel call* that was fully revealed in the coming of Jesus Christ as the Savior of the world.

Christian Calling

The third category of life's callings is our *Christian calling*. All Christians have a calling that motivates them to share Christ with the world through their lives and actions. Essentially, it involves becoming the hands, feet, and voice of Jesus ministering to the world. It inspires Christians with an inner sense of obligation to give back to others because of what Christ has done for them. Out of gratitude, they joyfully engage in the Lord's work on this earth. It includes much more than just going to church on Sunday and evangelizing, although that is included. It involves caring for the sick, caring for the orphans and widows, the poor, those in prison, and the list continues endlessly. This list is endless because the needs of our broken world are endless.

Special Call

Finally, the fourth category of life's callings is the *special call* of God. This is the call from God that leads people to devote their lives and careers to the work of ministry. This is what Paul experienced on his way to Damascus. It is what the prophets experienced when God called them to become His spokesmen and spokeswomen. It is what the apostles experienced when Jesus invited them to become His followers and later appointed the twelve as apostles. It is what ordination boards look for when they interview candidates for ordination. They are looking for people who recognize they are called to dedicate their lives to the work of ministry.

There is some debate within Christian circles about the last two categories—about whether we should distinguish between the general call to ministry that is given to all Christians and the special call to ministry given to members of the clergy. The question is raised, Does the Lord only call a select group of believers to lead His work, or are all Christians called to do His work? If all Christians are called, how do we differentiate between those who lead ministry as clergy and those who lead in specialized areas of the Lord's work, such as counselors, church administrators, and so on? What about the lay folk who dedicate their lives and careers to a specialized area in the Lord's work? If all Christians are called, is this distinction unhealthy for the church?

The way a person answers that question tends to shape their understanding of the special call to ministry and the ordination process. The prevalent understanding throughout church history is the Lord especially calls some individuals to leadership roles within the church, and this calling is recognized by the church through its ordination process.

The Words Call and Calling

One of the challenges that arise when discussing our *calling in life* or the *special call* to ministry is the broad usage of the simple words *call* and *calling*. *Webster's Dictionary* lists twenty-eight different types of usage for "call" when it is used as an intransitive verb and another forty-one times as a transitive verb. Additionally, it lists five categories of its usage as a noun (Webster 1996). This is also true of the equivalent words in both the Hebrew and Greek languages.

Biblical Words for "Call"

The Hebrew word for *call* is *qara* and occurs more than 730 times in the Old Testament. It is rarely used about animals (three times) but is primarily used "to draw someone's attention with the sound of the voice to establish contact." It is closely connected with the words *gana* (answer) and *schmck* (hear) and used to describe what happened when God called to Adam in the garden after he sinned: "Where are you?" (Genesis 3:9 NIV). In this instance, the Lord God is seeking to establish a relationship with him, and it should also be noted that many uses of *qara* occur when the Lord (Yahweh) is the subject and is calling "someone to be in service of Yahweh." In most of these instances, when the Lord (Yahweh) calls someone, He takes possession of them, proclaiming His sovereignty over them and the right to use them for His special service. This was the case with the young boy Samuel. In the middle of the night, "The LORD called Samuel" (1 Samuel 3:4 NIV) (VanGemeren 1997).

This Hebrew word is also connected with another Hebrew word that has a similar meaning but a stronger implication. This word includes accosting another person to get their attention. The scriptures provide us with several examples where this word is used to describe how the Lord called individuals into His service.

In the New Testament, the word most often translated as *call* is the Greek word *kale*. It appears almost 150 times in the New Testament and is translated as *call* in more than 125 of those instances. This Greek word has a meaning similar to the English word *call* and is used to describe how Jesus initially called His first disciples. Jesus's invitation was for Peter, Andrew, James, and John to follow him as disciples and embodied the essence of the gospel call. As these disciples continued to follow Jesus and were faithful and obedient to Him and His teachings, He chose twelve of them to become His apostles.

The Call of the First Disciples

The call of the first disciples is described in the early chapters of the Synoptic Gospels. Four of them were fishermen. Mark describes Jesus as walking by the Sea of Galilee and observing Peter and Andrew busy at work with their fishing business when He called them. "When he had gone a little farther, he saw James son of Zebedee and his brother John in a boat, preparing their nets. Without delay, *he called* them, and they left their father Zebedee in the boat with the hired men and followed him" (Mark 1:19–20 NIV). On that occasion, he promised to make them "fishers of men" (Mark 1:17 KJV).

Those fishermen could not have imagined all that lay ahead for them in those early days as His followers. But God did! Their decision to accept the simple invitation to become a disciple of this young rabbi launched them onto a career path that resulted in their being appointed as apostles and made pillars in the church. Ultimately, it meant having their names inscribed in the very foundations of the heavenly New Jerusalem. What began with a simple invitation was to ultimately become an eternal honor beyond their imagination. This is what can happen when a person answers the Lord's call!

The early steps of obedience taken in faith trusting the Lord to guide us to the next step can often lead to something much greater than initially imagined. As we obey His call and follow His leading, life often unfolds in both exciting and unbelievable ways. This certainly was the case with Jesus's twelve disciples.

I believe one of the key moments in the lives of the disciples came at the height of Jesus's ministry and was central to their understanding of their calling. Multitudes had gathered around Jesus, and on this occasion, He challenged His disciples to look upon the crowd and consider the people as a harvest field of humanity in need of workers (see Matthew 9:35–38). Jesus challenged His disciples to pray about the need for workers for the harvest. I believe that was a pivotal moment in the lives of the apostles. As they allowed this scene to penetrate their minds and hearts, they sensed with growing conviction the need to do something about the brokenness of people. It was soon after this occasion that Jesus appointed the twelve apostles and sent them on their first mission.

A young businessman shared with me an encounter he had with a retired minister near the end of his life. After a brief greeting in a restaurant, the retired minister challenged this young businessman to consider going into ministry. When the young businessman answered that he had prayed about it and did not believe the Lord was calling him into the ministry, the retired minister quickly responded, "You don't need to waste God's time praying about this; he's already given you the answer. Go read Matthew 9:35." That minister recognized that if this young man took seriously Jesus's words to pray about the need for workers in the Lord's harvest fields, it was likely that this young businessman would sense the Lord's voice calling him to go work in His harvest fields.

The Rhythm of Calling and Sending

It is interesting to note how two key Greek words used in the New Testament communicate the rhythm of the Lord's call. Those Greek words are *ekklēsia* and *apostello.* The first word, ekklēsia, is usually translated as "church."

The second word is translated as "apostle" and is simply a transliteration of this Greek word.

The first word, *ekklēsia*, is a compound Greek word made up of the preposition *ek,* which means *out* or *out of,* and the word *kaleo,* which means *to call.* This compound word means the *called-out ones* or the *called-together ones.* Many scholars believe the usage of the preposition *ek* indicates that believers are those who have been called out of the world and called unto Christ.

The second word, *apostello,* means apostle. This compound Greek word is made up of the Greek preposition *apo,* which means *from* or *out from,* and the verb *stello,* which, in this context, means *to be sent.* Thus, this Greek word means *the sent-out one.* This illustrates the rhythm of the call into ministry.

In sequence, these two Greek words suggest that Christians are first called to Christ to learn how to truly be His disciple, and then they are sent out to do His work. It is only after they have learned what it means to be a true follower of Christ that they are equipped for leadership roles in the church. Among those followers who are truly devoted to Him, the Lord chooses those He wills and calls them to lead His work.

Some disciples who began with Jesus quit somewhere along the way. We know this was true for the rich young ruler in Matthew 19. The cost of selling his possessions and following Jesus was too much of a price for him to pay. No doubt others lost interest in becoming a disciple when they discovered the cost of following Jesus. Some became distracted with the cares of life and stopped following Jesus. The call of God demands that our devotion to Jesus be the priority of our lives.

A Student's Story

One of my students shared the story of his journey to faith and calling to ministry this way. When he was in elementary school, his parents' divorce left him bitter over their split. In high school, his pain over their split led him to drinking and becoming a part of the party scene. A few months after graduation, 9/11 occurred, and in a spirit of patriotism, he enlisted in the military. During his time in the military, his drinking increased, and he started down a path toward becoming an agnostic. Eventually, he came to the place in which he described himself as an atheist.

After his discharge from the military, he returned home, found a good job, and began to pursue the American dream. However, the party scene and alcohol began to consume more and more of his life; over time, he realized that he was going nowhere fast. One evening after a weekend of parties, he began to reflect on his life and all the chaos around him. While he was reflecting on his life, he was prompted to seek the Lord and ask Him for help.

He relayed what happened. "I went into my bedroom, and knelt by my bed, and told the Lord, 'Jesus, if You are who they say You are, I need to know it, and I need to know now.'" He continued, "At that moment Jesus came into my room, and I began to weep before the Lord, confess my sins, and ask for forgiveness. When I got up from my knees, I was a different man. God had saved me. I felt as if a tremendous weight had been lifted off my shoulders, and everything seemed so new—even the trees and mountains!"

The following Sunday, he attended a church pastored by one of his friends from the gym. At the end of the service, he went forward to make a public profession of his newfound faith. After the service, he purchased a Bible. Before, when he attempted to read the Bible, it was always a chore, and he could never understand it. However, this time it was different—he could not put the Bible down. Over the next month, he read through all four of the Gospels in his tree stand while hunting. He described this period as being one of the happiest times of his life.

A couple of months after his experience that night, his interest in studying the Bible and theology grew to the point he considered attending a Bible college. However, he dismissed this idea as being only a remote possibility. A few weeks later, he was awakened in the middle of the night and felt the need to pray—it seemed as though the Lord was saying to him, "I want you to preach and teach the Bible."

At first, he shrugged off that impression as being nothing significant. However, the idea would not go away. A couple of weeks later, he told his father about his experience. His father told him to forget the idea—he would never be a preacher.

However, the idea would not go away. He went back to his father a second time, and again his father laughed at the idea of him becoming a preacher. A few weeks later, he went to his pastor. His pastor's reaction was just the opposite of his father's. His pastor was thrilled about the idea of him becoming a preacher and encouraged him to keep his mind open to the possibility of ministry. Soon after that conversation with his pastor, he enrolled in an online Bible college program. He planned to keep his dream job and prepare for a bivocational ministry.

Later, his pastor began a sermon series about "the crucified self." During that series in a Sunday-evening service, he experienced a moment in which he realized the Lord was calling him to dedicate his entire career to the work of ministry. That defining moment was the confirmation of his call. A few weeks later, his company began the process of downsizing, and he was laid off from his dream job. He recognized this as being the providential hand of the Lord in his life. Soon after, he relocated to a Christian college and enrolled in a ministry program. Is this typical of the special call of God?

Each Person Is Unique

When the Lord calls us, He knows our potential, our strengths, our weaknesses, our faults, our frailties, and our past failures. He takes all of this into consideration when He calls us. Each person is a unique creation of God and created in such a way that they have the potential to reflect to this world a tiny sliver of their Creator's image in a way that no other human being who has ever lived or who will ever live can reflect that image. In other words, after God made us, He threw away the pattern. This fact alone means that every human life has infinite value before God and is to be treasured and protected. Only God knows the potential that lies within each human being.

The conception of a human being does not take place without God's oversight. When Rachel complained to her husband, Jacob, that he would not give her children, he told her that God is the one who gives human life. He responded to her complaint, "Am I in the place of God, who has kept you from having children?" (Genesis 30:2 NIV).

God knows our potential from the moment of our conception. He watches over our development in the womb. David wrote, "I praise you because I am fearfully and wonderfully made; your works are wonderful, I know that full well. My frame was not hidden from you when I was made in the secret place when I was woven together in the depths of the earth. Your eyes saw my unformed body; all the days ordained for me were written in your book before one of them came to be" (Psalm 139:14–16 NIV). God perfectly understands our gifts, talents, abilities, interests, and personalities and knows how to call us to the work that He needs done on this earth.

Jeremiah discovered the time, location, and circumstance of his birth was no accident. God said to him, "Before I formed you in the womb I knew you before you were born I set you apart; I appointed you as a prophet to the nations" (Jeremiah 1:5 NIV). As we seek God's guidance in our lives and submit to His lordship, we discover that He faithfully guides us along the pathway of His calling. There are many times when we can see His providence at work as He calls us. We happen to be in the right place at the right time.

Hearing the Voice of Our Creator

While many voices are vying for our attention and seeking to call us in one direction or the other, the most important voice is the voice of our Creator. He is the one who invites us to find a new spiritual life in Him. He is the one who promises to walk with us throughout this journey of life and will faithfully guide us around life's pitfalls. He is the Good Shepherd who cares for His sheep and calls them by name. When we take the time to seek His leadership, we discover that He is faithful to help us sort through all the voices and impressions that are clamoring for our attention and steer us along the right path. It is the pathway of His calling.

Although we may have questions and doubts about our abilities and our insecurities, He faithfully guides us in the paths of effective service as we trust and obey His voice. We may be concerned about whether the right opportunities will come our way. However, over time, we discover that the right doors open for us at the right time. Pray this simple prayer: "Lord, help me to be at the right place, at the right time, doing the right thing, with the right people."

How Our Calling Comes

Followers of Christ can be sure that God works on our behalf to accomplish His purposes even when we do not always understand our circumstances.

The psalmist says, "The steps of a *good* man are ordered by the Lord, And He delights in his way" (Psalm 37:23 NKJV).

Sometimes the Lord takes even the bad circumstances of our lives and uses them to call us to His work. The scriptures teach, "That in all things God works for the good of those who love him, who have been called according to his purpose" (Romans 8:28 NIV). This was the case of the late Chuck Colson and his founding of Prison Fellowship Ministries. He went to prison because of his involvement in the Watergate scandal. However, while in prison, he came to know Christ, and soon God began to open his eyes to the suffering inside the prisons. As a result, he founded Prison Fellowship Ministries.

The circumstances we find ourselves in are often like a vector force pulling us in a particular direction. In those situations, God is faithful to guide us along the paths of His calling.

This was the case for John Walsh, founder of America's Most Wanted program. His career in helping track down criminals fleeing from justice began because of a tragedy in his own life—his young son was brutally murdered. As he sought consolation for his grief and searched to make meaning in his life, he discovered a new purpose in life—helping to track down criminals. As a result of his career, many grieving families of victims found a degree of consolation for their pain when the perpetrators of crimes were located and brought to justice.

One Step at a Time

When God calls us, often, rather than giving us a panoramic view of our future, He gives us only enough direction to take the next step. He does not overwhelm us with a lot of details about the future. Instead, He says, "Take my hand. Trust Me, and I will faithfully guide you through life's journey to your destination."

What we discover is that as each step is taken in obedience to His call, He gives us enough guidance for the next step. His providential leadership is more easily recognized as we look back on His faithfulness in the past rather than attempting to sort through our future. When we recall God's faithfulness in the past, we are inspired to trust Him for the future.

A few years ago, I was a part of a short-term missionary team that built a couple of churches in the Amazon jungle of Peru along the Maranon River. We crossed the Andes Mountains and traveled to the end of the road, got into a cargo boat, and traveled a hundred miles downriver to a small, primitive village of about three hundred people in a remote section of the jungle. The people lived in bamboo huts with thatched roofs and were isolated from the outside world except for the cargo boats that navigated the river. When night fell in the jungle, it was extremely dark, and people did not venture out of their huts without a flashlight.

When church services were held at night, the people walked together in small groups of about a half dozen people, with the leader holding a flashlight. The flashlight's beam only gave enough light for them to safely take the next step. They were able to safely navigate to the church and back to their homes with the light given by the flashlight's beam. They could not see the entire way home—only enough to take the next step. However, they were able to arrive safely at home by taking each step in the light. Often, that is the way it is with the journey of life. We are only given enough direction for the next step.

In the next four chapters, the four categories of life's callings are examined more in depth as we seek to gain a better understanding of the special call to ministry.

Questions for Thought and Reflection

1. What four categories of life's calling are identified in this chapter?
2. Briefly describe each category.
3. Read the story of the call of the disciples from the time of their first encounter with Jesus until He appointed them as apostles. (See Mark 1:16–20; Matthew 9:9, 35–38, 10:1–20; Mark 3:13–19; and Luke 6:12–16.)
4. What is the Greek word for church, and what does it mean?
5. What is the Greek word for an apostle, and what does it mean?
6. How are the two related to the Lord's call in our lives?"

Pascal, B. 2007. "The Heart-Shaped Vacuum That Can Only Be Filled by God." Vineyard Muses, September 14. Retrieved December 4, 2012. http://takmeng.blogspot.com/.

VanGemeren, W. A. 1997. *New International Dictionary of Old Testament Theology and Exegesis*, vol. 3. Grand Rapids: Zondervan.

Webster. 1996. *Webster's Encyclopedic Unabridged Dictionary of the English Language*. New York: Random House Value Publishing, Inc.

The Gospel Call

Many are called but few are chosen.
—Matthew 22:14 KJV

Introduction

What is the *gospel call* and where does it originate? This call is the most important calling in life we receive. Answering the gospel call is the only way for us to gain eternal life. We are born into this world alienated from God and in need of redemption. God's original purpose was for humanity to live in intimate fellowship with Him, experiencing spiritual life, peace, wholeness, and everlasting happiness. His intent was for the human family to live eternally in His presence.

The gospel call was not needed in the Garden of Eden because Adam and Eve lived in perfect fellowship with God. They were as spiritually alive as they could possibly be and designed to live eternally in His presence in paradise. This *gospel call* only became necessary because sin was introduced into the world. Adam and Eve's rebellion alienated them from God, brought about their spiritual death, and plunged humanity into the night of sin. Because of their sin, every member of humanity is born alienated from their Creator and in need of redemption.

To properly understand the gospel call, we begin with the story of the Fall and follow the Bible's storyline of how God unfolded His plan of redemption one step at a time. In examining His plan of redemption, we begin with the call of the patriarchs and follow with how God revealed His plan of redemption to the people of the Old Testament. We finally arrive at His perfect revelation—Jesus Christ.

The story of redemption involves two parties—the Caller and the called. God is the Caller, and the members of the human race are those who are called. It is God who first reaches out to us and invites us to trust Him for our salvation. Through grace, He gives us the power to respond to His call—we can accept His invitation to salvation, or we can reject Him and His offer of salvation.

Call in the New Testament

In the New Testament, both the words *call* and *calling* are used to describe how God draws people to Himself—He calls us. He calls us by first awakening us to our need for salvation and then extends to us the grace that enables us to respond to His invitation.

The Synoptic Gospels describe how Jesus gathered his first disciples around him—He called them. At Capernaum, he saw Matthew at his tax collection table and called him to become one of His disciples by saying, "Follow me" (Matthew 9:9 NIV). After being invited to become a disciple, Matthew held a feast and invited Jesus along with his tax-collector friends to a meal. When the religious leaders saw Jesus eating with tax collectors, they scorned Him for associating with sinners. However, Jesus pointed out where they were missing the mark, "For I have not come to call the righteous, but sinners" (Matthew 9:13 NIV). In this story, the word *call* is used to describe how Jesus invited people to become His disciples.

During the last week of his life, Jesus used parables to teach and illustrated how people are brought into the kingdom of heaven by telling the story of a wedding feast held by a king for his son. Many people were invited to the feast. However, several of them did not show up, so he sent his servants into the streets to invite others to fill the banquet hall. One person came not properly dressed for the wedding feast and was thrown out. Jesus concluded His parable with "Many are called but few are chosen" (Matthew 22:14 KJV).

In several of his letters, Paul uses the words *call* and *calling* to describe the call to salvation. He wrote to the new converts in Thessalonica, "We constantly pray for you, that our God may make you worthy of his calling" (2 Thessalonians 1:11 NIV). Later, he wrote to the Corinthian Church, "Brothers and sisters, think of what you were when you were called" (1 Corinthians 7:1 NIV). In his Ephesian letter, Paul wrote, "I pray that the eyes of your heart may be enlightened so that you may know the hope to which He has called you" (Ephesians 1:18 NIV). In all these instances, God is the one who calls people to salvation.

Peter uses *calling* in a similar manner. In his second letter he wrote, "Therefore, my brothers and sisters, make every effort to confirm your calling and election" (2 Peter 1:10 NIV). Other references in the Bible could be included, but this list illustrates how God is the Caller reaching out to us and inviting us to trust Him for our salvation. We now look at why we need salvation in the first place—it is because of the Fall.

Paradise

When God created humanity, they reflected His spiritual image, and in this state, Adam and Eve did not need redemption. They were as spiritually alive as they could be. Their fellowship with God was uninterrupted, natural, and filled to the brim with joy. They lived in an environment overflowing with God's presence and experienced unparalleled joy and fellowship with their Creator. Their first and only thoughts were to please their Creator, obey His commands, and enjoy Him forever. Their unconstrained impulses were continually focused on worshipping God and doing His will.

The Fall

After some time, and it is not known how long this period lasted, Satan, in the form of a beautiful animal, entered the garden and deceived Eve. He enticed her to taste the fruit God had forbidden humans to eat by suggesting that doing so would enable them to live on a higher level independently of God. She would be able to determine her destiny.

She fell for his lie and tasted the fruit, then seduced her husband to join with her in sin. It was this action that plunged humanity into the night of spiritual death and released into the world an unimaginable vortex of chaos and death.

Before that day, their lives in paradise were incredibly awesome! There were no diseases, no death, no dying, and no pain. They lived in an environment of maximum freedom and minimum restraint. Life was joyful and purposeful as they lived every day in perfect harmony with their Creator, with each other, and with all of creation. Their Creator planned for them to enjoy this environment forever. However, Adam and Eve's tragic choice destroyed their paradise.

They had been told by God not to eat fruit from the tree of the knowledge of good and evil or they would die. However, Satan raised doubt in Eve's mind that evil might be a better option for her than good. He suggested that she would discover something new and better if she threw off the lordship of her Creator and took over her life. His lie was "You will be like God, knowing good and evil" (Genesis 3:5 NIV).

Paradise Lost

The first pair could not have imagined all that would result from their disobedience. The act of eating the forbidden fruit transformed them but not in the way they expected. It plunged them into the night of spiritual death. Tragically, it destroyed their relationship with God, the source of their spiritual life. As a result of their sin, all their offspring would be born into this world alienated from God in spiritual death and need of redemption. "Just as sin entered the world through one man, and death through sin, and in this way death came to all people" (Romans 5:12 NIV).

The spiritual death that Adam passed on to his offspring was so total that no member of the human race can find their way back to Creator without help. We must have God's help to find salvation. The only hope for humanity is salvation through Jesus Christ.

Fellowship with God Is Broken

Adam's greatest loss was his intimate fellowship with God. Humans are created to live in intimate fellowship with God and worship Him. The Fall created a spiritual void in the human heart that only God can fill. We are born with an insatiable desire to know God. Augustine referred to this disease when he said, "Thou hast made us for thyself, and our heart is restless until it finds its rest in thee" (Augustine, *Confessions*). Blaise Pascal, a seventeenth-century French mathematician and philosopher, said it this way, "There is a God-shaped vacuum in the heart of every man which cannot be filled by any created thing, but only by God, the Creator, made known through Jesus" (Pascal 2007). All of humanity is restless and searching to fill this void in their hearts until they find Christ.

Before their sin, Adam and Eve's time with their Creator was a time of unimaginable joy. Now the very sound of His presence in the garden struck fear in them as they sought to hide from Him and cover their bodies with fig leaves. They had been robbed of their innocence, their peace, joy, freedom, and relationship with their Creator.

Tragically, that void is often filled with evil instead of good. It took humans only one generation for the unimaginable to occur—a man to kill his brother. The tragedy of the Sandy Hook Elementary School shooting occurred on December 12, 2012, in Newtown, Connecticut. Twenty six- and seven-year-old school children and six of their teachers were killed by a deranged twenty-year-old gunman. At the time, many in the news media were attempting to understand this horror. They rightly concluded that it happened because of evil in the world. This tragedy can be traced back to what happened in the garden when sin was introduced to the human heart.

In the past few years, I have had students from Sierra Leon, Africa, who came to this country as refugees from the civil war that took place in that country in the 1990s. Three of them were captured by rebel soldiers and lived through the carnages of a civil war. They witnessed fellow citizens being lined up and randomly shot or having one of their arms or legs chopped off with machetes.

They now cherish life and live with gratitude that they survived those atrocities but must deal with images of witnessing the personification of evil. One student told how, in the terror of those moments, he saw men lose all control of their bodily functions. Another student, who was just five years old at the time, shared that he was not allowed to shed any tears. If he had shed even a single tear, they would have killed him. To this day, he is unable to express his emotions. Adam's sin had much worse consequences than he could have imagined.

The Imprint of Paradise Remains

What has remained in human conscientiousness is a trace of what it must have been like to live in paradise. Innately, we know this world should be a better place than it is. But try as we may, we are unable to restore this world to a paradise. Even those who are wealthy or famous and have access to material wealth and power experience relationship problems, separations, illnesses, death, and other tragedies that painfully remind them they are living in a fallen world. John Milton's *Paradise Lost* is about the imprint of paradise left on the soul.

All the sickness, hurt, death, and destruction in this world can be traced back to the destructive forces unleashed by Adam's sin. Instead of paradise, we now live with the harsh realities of a world filled with pain, disease, heartache, separation, and death. The incredible hope of the Gospel is that, in the end, when our redemption is complete, everything will be restored to the paradise it was originally, and once again we will be able to live in harmony with God, one another, and all of creation.

God's Call in the Garden

After Adam and Eve's sin, the Lord God came walking through the garden and called out to them, "Where are you?" (Genesis 3:9 NIV). God was not inquiring about their location. He is all-knowing and knew their physical location. What He was saying to them was, "What happened to you? Where are you spiritually?" Their sin had alienated them from Him, and for the first time in their lives, they realized what it was like to be cut off from the source of their spiritual life and attempted to hide from Him.

In response to their sin, the first sacrifice in the Bible is offered and represents a foreshadowing of the gospel call. God took the skin of an animal to provide a covering for them. The cost for that covering was an animal's life, which involved the shedding of blood. The Hebrew writer wrote, "Without the shedding of blood there is no forgiveness" (Hebrews 9:22 NIV). Because of the price of redemption, the Hebrew writer calls our salvation "so great a salvation" (Hebrews 2:3 NIV). The only way we can be reconciled to God is through the blood of Christ.

Original Sin

The theological term for this spiritual death in humanity is *original sin*. Humans cannot find their way back to God by their efforts. They must have outside help. From beginning to end, salvation is the work of God provided for us through Jesus Christ. He is the one who initiates the call, and His grace enables us to seek Him. To even hear God's voice, we must first be awakened to our spiritual death and need of salvation through God's prevenient grace. It is God who awakens us through the voice of the Holy Spirit and invites us to trust Christ for salvation.

Each semester, I have my students write about their journey of faith. For me, it is one of the most important papers they write. I tell them, after I have read their stories, they have a new professor, and I have a new class. Instead of merely seeing faces and learning their names, I see stories. I see the pain, struggle, disappointments, betrayals, and questions my students have as they search for meaning and purpose in their lives.

One of my students described her spiritual journey in this manner.

At the time of her conversion, she was enrolled in a state college and unhappy with life. One day, she began to pray for God to show her that He exists. Following her prayer that night, the very next day on campus, she ran into a guy carrying a sign that read, "If you died today, where would you spend eternity?" Immediately, she recognized that God was answering her prayer.

However, she was not ready to yield her life to Christ's lordship. A few days later, after a weekend of partying, while listening to the evening news, she became very distraught with world events and retreated to her room to think about what was going on in her life and the world. She prayed for the Lord to forgive her sins and come into her life. During that moment, she felt the burden of her sins lifted and the peace of God filling her heart. She described this as a time of tremendous joy.

In a little while, her mother became worried and went to her room to check on her. When her mother first saw her, she realized something had happened and remarked, "You have been saved." She saw that her countenance was different.

She discovered a new joy in reading the Bible and would often read it into the wee hours of the morning. She also discovered joy in attending church and being with other Christians. Her life was transformed by God's redeeming grace, and she was now alive in Christ.

The First Sacrifices

In the story of the Fall, it was not long before the first human pair witnessed a tragic event because of their sin—one of their sons killed his brother. Because God's method of providing a covering involved the sacrifice of an animal, it was recognized that God's forgiveness requires sacrifice. Adam and Eve's two sons, Cain and Abel, both brought sacrifices to worship the Lord. Abel brought an animal sacrifice, while Cain brought a grain offering. The Lord accepted Abel's sacrifice but rejected Cain's. (See Genesis 4.) We are not sure why the Lord did not accept Cain's sacrifice. Both animal sacrifices and grain offerings were a part of the Levitical sacrificial system in the Old Testament. The scriptures simply tell us that

Able brought the best of his flock. Did Cain hold back the best of his grain for himself?

Because the Lord accepted Abel's sacrifice and rejected his, Cain became jealous and sought to even the score of his perceived injustice. He caught Abel in the field and killed him. What Cain quickly discovered was that his sin only exacerbated his problem rather than solving it. First, the Lord called for him to give an account for his brother. The Lord asked Cain, "Where is your brother Abel?" (Genesis 4:9 NIV) and followed with "What have you done? Listen! Your brother's blood cries out to me from the ground" (Genesis 4:10 NIV).

Cain discovered that now the whole earth was against him. "You will be a restless wanderer on the earth" (Genesis 4:12 NIV). It was so bad that Cain found it wearisome to even continue with life, to the point that he now needed God's mercy just to live.

Old Testament Altars

As the Bible's storyline continues, the world became so evil that God had to destroy it with a deluge of water. However, in mercy, He spared Noah, his family, and the animal kingdom. After the Flood, Noah built an altar and offered a clean animal in sacrifice as he worshipped God, who had spared him. The Genesis story continues with Abraham, Isaac, and Jacob all building altars to worship the Lord.

Following the Lord's call, Abraham relocated to Palestine and built an altar. Later, he built at least three other altars. (See Genesis 12:8; 13:18; 22:9.) It seems that wherever Abraham settled, he built an altar. Isaac followed his father's example and built an altar in Beersheba. (See Genesis 26:25.) After acquiring his wives, family, and flocks in Haran, Jacob returned to Bethel, where once again he was met by God and built an altar. (See Genesis 35:7.) The altar was a special place for these men as they offered their sacrifices and worshipped God.

The Israelites

Centuries later, after leaving Egypt, when the Israelites arrived at Mount Sinai, Moses was called to the top of Mount Sinai and given the Ten Commandments along with the blueprint for the Tabernacle. He was instructed to place an altar in front of the Tabernacle where the people could bring their sacrifices as they worshipped the Lord. Throughout the Old Testament, animal sacrifices were an integral part of worship at both the Tabernacle and later temples.

However, neither the altar nor its sacrifices could sufficiently atone for sin. They simply represented a foreshadowing of the perfect sacrifice. When Jesus Christ shed his blood and died on the cross, He was the perfect atonement for sin. When He said, "It is finished" (John 19:30 NIV) and died, the atonement for sin was completed. His death makes it possible for every human being to be forgiven of their sins and be reconciled to their Creator—to have eternal life through Jesus Christ.

The Perfect Revelation

Jesus's life, ministry, death, and resurrection for the redemption of the fallen human race provides the pathway whereby we can be reconciled to God. Jesus came to earth to save sinners and restore them to fellowship with their Creator. Paul pointed this out when he wrote that Jesus came into this world "to save sinners—of whom I am the worst" (1 Timothy 1:15 NIV). This is the *gospel call*, and evangelicals teach that this salvation involves a transformative element called *the new birth.*

The New Birth

When Nicodemus asked Jesus about the way to heaven, he was perplexed by Jesus's answer. Jesus answered him, "Very truly I tell you, no one can see the kingdom of God unless they are born again" (John 3:3 NIV). Nicodemus was confused; this made no sense to him. It is not until a person has experienced the transformative work of the new birth that Jesus's answer makes sense to them.

Salvation begins when God reaches out to us with His awakening grace. We are so spiritually dead that without outside help, we do not recognize that we need to be saved. On their own, the greatest wise men of the world have been unable to find the path to reconciliation with God. Through dedication and discipline, they have sought to penetrate the darkness and find their way to enlightenment and eternal life, but with all their efforts, they have only discovered a shadow of the truth.

The fact that we are unable to save ourselves is borne out in Paul's letter to the Ephesian believers. He wrote about their pre-conversion days, "You were dead in your transgressions and sins" [and you were] "without hope and without God" (Ephesians 2:1, 12 NIV). He then goes on to explain that "God, who is rich in mercy, made us alive with Christ even when we were dead in transgressions—it is by grace you have been saved" (Ephesians 2:4–5 NIV). The scriptures are very clear about the source of our salvation. Salvation is God's gift of grace to us.

Prevenient Grace

John Wesley, the founder of the Methodist Church, taught that the awakening of our conscience to our sin and alienation from God and the need for salvation is God's prevenient grace. God first reaches out to us and lifts us to the level where we can respond to His invitation to salvation. Wesley taught that this prevenient grace is made possible through the sacrificial death of Christ and that on some level, God's prevenient grace is given to every person on earth.

Saving Faith

The conversion process begins with the awakening work of the Holy Spirit and culminates with the new birth, in which we are raised to new spiritual life in Christ. From beginning to end, salvation is the work of God's saving grace and is referred to as the *gospel call*. It is singularly the most important call that we receive in this life. Without this call, we will continue in spiritual death that eventually results in eternal death. This call begins when a person is awakened to their sin and need of redemption by God. Conversion happens when they respond to God's invitation by repenting of their sins and trusting Jesus as their Lord and Savior; they are raised through grace to new spiritual life in Christ. Thus, from beginning to end, salvation is the work of God's grace raising us to a new relationship with our Creator.

On the cross, when Jesus cried out, "It is finished" (John 19:30 NIV), the work of redemption was complete. Through Jesus Christ, we can now be forgiven of our sins and justified. Through the power of the Spirit, it is now possible for us to walk in a new life in Christ and to possess the hope of eternal life.

Vibrant Faith Is Essential to Understanding the Special Calling

A vibrant, growing relationship with Jesus Christ is essential to clearly understand the *special call* to ministry. Confusion about God's call to ministry can often be traced back to an anemic faith. When our walk with the Lord is erratic, hampered by repeated failures, lapses of faith, and disobedience, confusion often arises about what God is calling us to do. The best way to clearly understand the call to ministry is by cultivating and maintaining a vibrant relationship with Christ.

We now turn our attention to another category of life's calling—the *vocational call*. This call was given to Adam and Eve while they were living in paradise, before they sinned.

Questions for Thought and Reflection

1. List as many of the elements of God's image as you can think of that were reflected in humans when God created us. (See Genesis 1:26.)
2. Why was no clothing necessary for humans before the Fall? (See Genesis 2:23; 3:7,10–11.)
3. List as many of the effects of the Fall on humanity as you can. (See Genesis 3:14–19; Romans 5:12–19.)
4. What prompted Noah to build an altar after the Flood?

5. What prompted Abraham to build his altars in Palestine (Genesis 12:1–9)?
6. Who/what awakens us to our need for salvation?
7. Describe the new birth.
8. What is prevenient grace?

Pascal, B. 2007. "The Heart-Shaped Vacuum That Can Only Be Filled by God. " Vineyard Muses, September 14. Retrieved December 4, 2012. http://takmeng.blogspot.com/.

The Vocational Call

Be fruitful and increase in number; fill the earth and subdue
it. Rule over the fish in the sea and the birds in the sky and
over every living creature that moves on the ground.
—Genesis 1:28 (NIV)

Work that engages our minds, challenges our physical stamina and creative
skills, and utilizes our talents is a noble calling. It is part of the created
order of the universe. After God created humanity, He gave the first
pair work to do. In their paradise, Adam and Eve had plenty of work to
challenge them, and they enjoyed it! When our redemption is complete, we
too will have work to do in the new heaven and new earth. This chapter
is about our *vocational calling*.

Work that engages the mind of the scientist who seeks to unlock the secrets of the universe to make this world a better place for humanity, whether it is in medicine, science, or another field, is noble. Francis Collins referred to his work as a physician and scientist as his calling. He recognized his vocational calling before he became a Christian. He was chosen to lead the international team that worked on the Human Genome Project and pioneered mapping the human DNA.

While reflecting on his career as a physician and scientist in a lecture at Cal Tech, he described his youth as a time when he was "at best an agnostic or more likely an atheist." But it was also during this period of life that he discovered his calling. He started college as a physics major, then switched to a chemistry major, and then switched again to a biology major, and finally ended up in medicine. His decision to go into medicine was the time when he discovered his *real calling* in life (Dallas Willard 2010).

The *vocational call* is an inner motivation that calls a person to engage in social, civic, and occupational activities that make this earth a more hospitable place in which to live. It involves taking care of the earth and giving our best efforts to our work. God told Adam to take care of the garden and subdue the earth. This calling was given to humanity while they were living in paradise and before they sinned.

During medieval times, the word *vocation* was used exclusively to refer to the work of clergy (Richard Taylor 1983). However, over time it took on a broader meaning that included secular employment, especially the helping professions, and is frequently used both within as well as outside Christian circles.

It causes a person to pursue one line of work over another. It is like a vector force that draws a person toward one type of occupation and is linked with a person's gifts, talents, interests, experiences, abilities, and opportunities in life.

While the *vocational call* does not receive the same amount of attention in the scriptures as the *Christian calling* or the *special call*, nevertheless it has an important place in the Bible and is vitally linked to our responsibilities as Christians.

In the secular world, the expression *one's calling in life* is frequently used to refer to a person's vocational employment. People who enjoy their line of work and are fulfilled by it often refer to their occupations as their calling.

34

Many teachers, doctors, nurses, businessmen, and others, especially in the helping professions, enthusiastically do their work with a sense of calling. Others, such as engineers, mechanics, pilots, and accountants, find varying degrees of satisfaction and fulfillment in their work. They discover they are naturally suited for one line of work and not another and are affirmed as they give their best efforts in their work. Because of their work, this world is a better place to live.

Captain Chesley Sullenberger, an airline pilot, spent many years flying airliners and safely transporting passengers from one destination to another. One day while taking off from New York's La Guardia Airport and climbing toward his cruising altitude, he struck a flock of geese, destroying his engines. On board were 123 passengers along with crew members. His quick thinking and skilled reaction to this accident enabled him to glide his airplane down to a crash landing on the Hudson River saving the lives of everyone on board.

This remarkable feat was attributed to his skills as an airline pilot. Many of his passengers on board the airplane that day joined him a year later in an anniversary flight to celebrate their *Miracle on the Hudson*. Few would question Captain Sullenberger's skills as an airline pilot. This world is a better place because of the remarkable skill of this pilot—especially the people and families of those on board his airplane that day!

Although vocation is often thought of in secular terms and attributed to personal interests, it does have spiritual connections and was an integral part of God's plan at creation. Our work ethic and habits should reflect devotion to our Creator. They are related to who we are as God's image-bearers. As Christians, we ought to seek the Lord's guidance in our vocational employment as well as all our other choices in life. Our Creator is interested in how we spend our time on this earth.

In a TV interview with Sean Hannity, Jose Rodriguez discussed his work as the head of a branch of the Central Intelligence Agency (CIA) during the Iraq and Afghanistan wars. In that interview, Rodriguez described his passion for his work in this manner, "I felt called to protect the American people" (Rodriguez, 2012).

Where did this calling come from? Who called him to protect the American people? No doubt he went through a similar screening and training process as all the other CIA employees. The trajectory of his career most likely followed a similar path as many others in the CIA. In what sense could he describe his work as being a calling?

While the gospel call was given in response to Adam's sin, the vocational call was embedded in the created order. The gospel call has its origin in God's grace. The vocational call has its origin in creation. Just as the gospel call is extended to every person, so the vocational call is given to every member of the human family. Everyone is called to be a productive member of their community. Through our vocational work, we are called to take care of the earth and make it a better place for humans to inhabit.

Sometimes it is easy to fall into the error of thinking that God is only interested in the spiritual aspects of life. That kind of thinking is a mistake. God is vitally interested in all aspects of life, even taking note of the sparrow that falls to the ground. (See Matthew 10:29.) If something as small as a sparrow is important to God, then all our time spent on this earth is important to Him, including our vocational work.

Adam's First Call—His Vocational Calling

God created Adam as the vice-regent of the earth and called him to be a steward of the earth's resources. This calling continues with humanity throughout history, summoning us to protect and preserve the earth from unnecessary and reckless destruction. This mandate also calls us to give the best efforts in our vocational work, whether that work is secular or sacred. In all our work, we should seek to bring glory to our Creator—even when we are working at tasks that we do not particularly enjoy.

Adam's vocational call is summarized in the first two chapters of Genesis. God instructed Adam to rule over the earth, to fill the earth with his offspring, to take care of the garden, to till the land, to subdue the earth, and to name the animals. As God's image-bearer, Adam was to use his physical strength, intellectual abilities, and creative talents to take care of God's creation. There are a couple of observations about work and our vocational calling that are borne out in the creation story.

First, Adam's vocational call provided him with plenty of physical and mental challenges. His work of cultivating the garden, naming the animals, and subduing the earth challenged him both physically and mentally. Taking care of the garden involved physical work. Naming the animals presented a mental challenge. "By naming the animals, Adam demonstrated mastery over them" (Walton, Matthews and Chavalas 2000).

We are not sure of what exactly was meant by subduing the earth. Presently it includes seeking to overcome and eradicate diseases, anticipating and preparing for natural disasters, and battling hostile forces that threaten the quality of our lives. God expects humans to work toward making this world a more hospitable environment in which to live and work.

Second, we are called to be creative in our work. Our vocational work should unleash our artistic, intellectual, and creative talents. Just as God created this world, similarly, we are called to be creative in how we go about taking care of the earth. This involves discovering our gifts, talents, abilities, and interests and then using them to bless our families and neighbors. It involves taking advantage of the opportunities that come our way to make our world a better place.

Vocation and Calling

The English word *vocation* is a transliteration of the Latin word *vocare,* which simply means *to call.* As pointed out earlier, in its early usage, it had strong religious connotations and described the work of a minister. However, over time, its usage expanded to describe one's occupation, and now it is often used to describe one's secular occupation.

Frederick Beuchner wrote, "Vocation happens when our deep gladness meets the world's deep need" (Buechner 1973). God designed us to be skilled at some tasks and not at others. Some occupations by their very nature interest us, while others have no appeal to us.

Fill the Earth

When the Lord said to the first pair, "Be fruitful and multiply and fill the earth" (Genesis 1:28 NIV), He called for them to produce offspring. The gift of procreation is both an awesome privilege and tremendous responsibility. Angels cannot procreate. In our resurrected bodies, we will no longer be able to procreate. However, in their created state, Adam and Eve and the rest of humanity were instructed to produce offspring.

To be able, with your marriage partner, to procreate another person, who in some sense bears your personal and physical image, is an incredible privilege. The family structure provides the context for the most intimate community relationships that exist on earth. Those relationships provide the contexts for life's greatest blessings of a family and home.

In addition to continuing the human race, children carry on family traditions and heritages and pass them along to their children. Culture and life philosophies are passed through succeeding generations by the family. The scriptures teach that the righteous choices of parents are a blessing for a thousand generations. On the other hand, sinful choices are a curse lasting even to the fourth generation. When giving the law to the Israelites in Exodus, the Lord said to them, "I, the Lord your God, am a jealous God, punishing the children for the sin of the parents to the third and fourth generation of those who hate me, but showing love to a thousand generations of those who love me and keep my commandments" (Exodus 20:5–6 NIV).

One day in class, I mentioned this verse, and many of my students immediately objected. They said, "This is not fair. I should not have to pay for the sins of my parents. I don't believe that God does that to us."

As I stood there searching for an answer, I was prompted to ask if anyone in the room felt they had been robbed of something because of their parents' divorce. The room quickly grew quiet as they realized that the choices of their parents had either blessed them or robbed them of something in life.

Righteous choices are a blessing to succeeding generations in ways that are beyond our ability to comprehend, while sinful choices rob our offspring of these blessings. I found it both fascinating and humbling that when my ancestors homesteaded in Indiana a couple of hundred years before I was born, they donated part of their land for a church.

A couple of generations later, one of my great-grandfathers married the preacher's daughter. Thus, generations before my birth, the blessings of their righteous choices were in some strange sense passed along to me in ways that I cannot fully comprehend.

Marriage and the home are integral to God's created order. The Bible begins with a wedding in the garden and ends with a wedding in heaven.

A society that successfully produces good marriages invariably causes its people to flourish. On the other hand, irreparable damage is caused when the institution of marriage is assaulted and the home undermined through cohabitation, same-sex covenants, and similar sinful choices.

Often children are the ones who suffer the most when the home is destroyed by divorce. They are robbed of the heritage God planned for them. When the marriage covenant is honored through faithfulness and covenant-keeping, the offspring produced by that relationship are blessed in a multitude of ways. When the vow is broken, children are shortchanged.

Subdue the Earth

In the creation story, God commanded Adam to subdue the earth. He was to "rule over the fish of the sea and the birds of the sky, and over every living thing that moves on the earth" (Genesis 1:28 NIV). What was involved in "subduing the earth" is not altogether clear. Likely, subduing the earth called for Adam to use his creative skills and talents as vice-regent to gain mastery over the earth and its animal kingdom. It may have included the challenge of making that part of the earth outside of the Garden of Eden an extension of the garden.

Sometimes this call is referred to as our cultural mandate. John Stott describes it this way: "For what God has given us is nature, whereas what we do with it is culture" (Stott, The Radical Disciple 2010). It is this cultural mandate that causes civilizations to develop and flourish. For example, many areas in the western United States were originally arid and for all practical purposes uninhabitable. However, with water storage, conservation, and irrigation, people now live comfortably in those areas.

All work that makes this world a better place in which to live is a noble occupation. Our Creator designed us to use our creative and intellectual skills to subdue those less desirable and uninhabitable parts of the earth and make them a more suitable environment in which to work and live. When we take on these challenges, it causes us to thrive.

Cultivate the Land

Another mandate of the vocational calling was to "cultivate it (the garden) and keep it" (Genesis 2:15 NIV). In his garden paradise, Adam had work to do! What did the call to cultivate the garden involve?

While it was Adam's paradise, it probably needed his attention to enhance its beauty and the environment. Perhaps he was challenged to develop his horticultural skills and grow even sweeter fruit or experiment with flowers producing new shades of radiant colors and exotic aromas. Maybe it involved doing something like farmers do today by developing better planting and fertilizing techniques to increase their yield and raise a better quality of grain.

At any rate, Adam's work affirmed him as vice-regent of the earth and called for him to use his physical strength, mental aptitude, creative skills, and artistic abilities to take care of the world. Os Guinness points out how this principle affected the life of one of his ancestors. It was the enthusiasm of a young farmer plowing his field that saved his great-great-grandmother from suicide and gave him a chance at life.

When his great-great-grandmother was an eighteen-year-old mother with two small children, her husband was foolishly killed in a shooting duel. The man who killed her husband deeply regretted it and offered to provide financially for her and the children. She refused his offer, choosing rather to face a life of poverty without much hope of her situation ever improving. A few months later, she sank into such despair that she decided the only way out was to take her life.

On the day she decided to carry out her plans, she walked to a nearby river, intending to jump off the bridge. However, when she got to the bridge, before she could carry out her plans, her eyes caught sight of a young farmer, about her same age, on the other side of the river, plowing his field.

What amazed her was the way he was doing his work. He was not plowing his field in just any manner to get the job done. Instead, he was making a piece of artwork out of his plowing. She watched with amazement as the young farmer created a piece of artwork with his plow.

She began to contemplate how this young farmer was able to transform such a mundane task into a powerfully creative moment. As she reflected on her own life, she concluded that if this young man could find meaning and purpose in such a common task as plowing a field, then she could find meaning and purpose in her life as the mother of two young children.

She rejected her thoughts of suicide and returned to her children with a renewed purpose and zest for life. She later married the world-famous distiller who bears the family name and bore more children. She made it her practice to pray each day for her children, for their children yet to be born, and for the future generations of her offspring. Os Guinness attributes his being a Christian apologist in part to her prayers (Guinness 1998).

Name the Animals

Another mandate in the Genesis account was for Adam to name all the animals and all birds. "He (God) brought them to the man to see what he would name them; and whatever the man called each living creature, that was its name" (Genesis 2:19 NIV). Naming all the animals was no small feat. The Hebrew word used in this context means to assign a name to an object that reflects its inherent qualities. Scientists estimate there are about eight thousand species of amphibian animals on earth and between nine and ten thousand species of birds. In the Hebrew language, assigning a person or object a name required for it to first be examined to discover its inherent qualities and then assigned the appropriate name. Identifying the inherent characteristics of all the animals before assigning them names would have given Adam a substantial intellectual challenge.

In conclusion, Adam was assigned familial, administrative, physical, and intellectual work to do. All of this happened before he sinned! There are a couple of observations that can be made from the creation story.

Work Is Not Punishment for Sin

First, work is not a punishment for sin. When God called Adam to subdue the earth, name the animals, till the land, and rule over the earth, he was living in paradise—the Garden of Eden! With Eden being a paradise, Adam certainly enjoyed his work. Indeed, sin has now complicated our work and often makes it toilsome. Now we live by the sweat of our brow, and thorns now infest the ground, complicating our work and diminishing the harvest. However, there is no place in the Bible that teaches that work in and of itself is the punishment for sin.

One day, one of my professors in seminary casually remarked, "I love my work. I look forward to coming to work every day." And then he added in jest, "There ought to be some kind of sin in that." On the contrary, fulfillment and affirmation from our work are what Adam experienced every day in the garden before sin destroyed his paradise. He began each day looking forward to his work and ended the day fulfilled and affirmed by his activities.

The Bible's depiction of Adam and Eve living in paradise is an indication of what our future occupation will be in our redeemed state. In the new heaven and new earth, with resurrected bodies, we will live in an incorruptible earth. What an incredible hope for the Christian!

During the first three hundred years of the church, the resurrection of the body was a key element of Christian hope. The early Christians envisioned that their resurrected bodies would resemble their physical bodies when they were at the peak of their physical strength and beauty—when they were in their twenties.

Tom Wright in *Surprised by Hope* points out that there will be work for us to do with our resurrected bodies in the new earth. Forget those images about lounging around playing harps. There will be work to do, and we shall relish doing it. All the skills and talents we have put to God's service in this present life—and perhaps, too, the interests and likings we gave up because they conflicted with our vocation—will be enhanced and ennobled and given back to us to be exercised to his glory (Wright 2008). God created us to enjoy our work.

Stewardship of the Earth

Second, God has entrusted humanity with the stewardship of the earth. Adam was instructed to cultivate the garden. As we enjoy the majesty of God's creation and hear Him speaking to us in a million ways through

His creation, we should recognize our responsibility to be good stewards of the earth.

A few years ago, I accompanied a group of college students on a concert tour. As we were traveling from one church to the next, we decided to take a shortcut over a mountain. What we did not realize when we left the main highway was that the shortcut was filled with a lot of switchbacks and harrowing turns. Just before we reached the summit of the mountain, we arrived at a spot that offered us a panoramic view of the valley floor. The beauty of that spot was so breathtaking that we stopped for pictures and then found it hard to leave because of its beauty. Our Creator has filled this world with such grandeur that at times it leaves us in awe and wonderment over His creation.

There is a lot of discussion today about the need to take care of our earth. It is sometimes challenging to sort through all these views to find the proper balance. Some tend to elevate the human obligation of taking care of our environment above the need to take care of people. Others go so far as to hold animal life on an almost equal level with human beings. What should be the Christian's attitude toward our environment?

John Stott gives three guidelines of how Christians ought to relate to this earth. First, Christians "must avoid the deification of nature and not make the mistake of the pantheist." Second, Christians "must avoid the opposite extreme and avoid the exploitation of nature." We are not to behave arrogantly as if we were God. Third, the proper relationship is "one of cooperation with God" (Stott, The Radical Disciple 2010). We are the caretakers of this world. Someone has remarked that every time a species becomes extinct, a part of God's fingerprints is erased. Christians are called to take care of this earth as good stewards of what God created for us to enjoy.

Dave Brookless lists three views that it is possible to take: "The first is the anthropocentric view that says the world is here for human use and enjoyment ... The second is the ecocentric view that sees humans as simply one part of an interdependent biosphere, with no greater rights than any other part. The third is the theocentric view that sees the world (human and non-human) as deriving its value from being created and sustained by God." He advocates the third view (Bookless 2008).

He goes on to develop his theology of sustainability on three pillars.

The first pillar is that we are to worship God as both "Creator and sustainer" of the earth.

The second pillar is God's covenant with humanity. In Genesis, God told Adam to till the soil. (See Genesis 3:23.) In the account of the Flood, the animal kingdom was gathered into the ark along with Noah and his family. This indicates the significance of animal life to God. After the Flood, God made a covenant with all the earth (including the animal kingdom) that He would never again destroy this earth with a flood and marked this covenant with the rainbow.

The third pillar is what he calls the creation-fall-redemption paradigm. It is through Jesus Christ that God has redeemed this world, and in the end, when redemption is complete, He will restore this earth to its final redeemed state (Bookless 2008).

When corporate greed depletes the earth of its resources, it robs future generations of those benefits, and Christians ought to be concerned. Years ago, one of the roads that I traveled back to school following a college break wound through an area that had been ravaged by strip mines, leaving behind a scarred wasteland. The area before the stretch of strip mines and the area on the other side of the strip mines were fields of farmland producing crops and supporting agriculture.

In the middle were thousands of acres that had been ravaged by strip mines and left behind as a virtual wasteland. That wasteland is a testimony to corporate greed that robbed future generations of its natural beauty and resources.

While it is true that in God's redemptive process this earth will be destroyed by fire (see 2 Peter 3:10), in the end, there will be a new earth that has been restored to its original beauty of a paradise. For the present time, our vocational calling is to take care of our earth as good stewards.

Work Affirms the Individual

Third, work affirms the individual. We are the bearers of our Creator's image. While the spiritual part of His image was marred by the Fall, we retain a shadow of His image. After each phase of God's work of creating this world and the animals, God evaluated His work with the assessment that "it was good" (Genesis 1:10, 12, 18, 21, and 25 NIV). However, when He created humanity, He evaluated it as "it was very good" (Genesis 1:31 NIV). God looked upon His creation with joy and delight. We, too, should look upon our work with joy and delight.

R. Paul Stevens discusses how God's creative image is reflected in our vocational calling. He includes a list of verbs the Bible uses to identify the work the Lord has called us to do: making, adorning, separating, organizing, cultivating, beautifying, improving, fixing, redeeming, renovating, informing, announcing, revealing outcomes, healing breaches, making peace, helping, sustaining, being with, communicating worth, celebrating, expressing joy, making beautiful things, imagining, dealing with evil, designing, planning, enlisting, empowering, consummating, entertaining, welcoming, providing a contest, showing hospitality, serving, and bringing to a conclusion (Stevens 1999).

At work one day, my wife asked a retired nurseryman about the secret to his success in the nursery business. He thought for a moment and then told her that early in his career, he developed the habit that after he planted a tree or put any plant in the ground, he would stop for a moment and pray, asking the Lord to make it grow. He concluded that habit, more than anything else, had contributed to his success in the nursery business.

When we see our work as an opportunity to partner with God and bring glory to Him, it adds purpose and significance to our work. We should do our work with zest and passion. As Christians, we should offer up to God our vocational work as a sacrifice of praise.

Luther

During the Reformation, Luther emphasized the priesthood of all believers, and the idea began to take root that our vocational work is important to God. The Puritans further developed the idea and concluded that every person is called to their vocational work by God. This caused vocational work to take on a more significant meaning among the Puritans and included the vocational work of nonclergy individuals.

Luther sought to elevate both the importance and significance of the laity. He was disturbed about dividing Christians into two categories: the clergy, who were the spiritually elite, and the laity, who were second-class Christians. He opposed this view and taught the priesthood of all believers, seeking to elevate the status of the laity.

According to Luther, the person whose vocational call was to be a farmer is just as much worshipping God by plowing his field as the preacher is by delivering a sermon on Sunday morning. God needs to have both tasks accomplished and uses people to do His work. Likewise, the mother who takes care of her home, washing the dishes, is as much carrying out the work of God as the clergyperson visiting the sick. God needs both people to do their work.

The Puritans

The Puritans carried this idea even further. Along with Luther, they sought to elevate the work of the common person and stressed that God's call applied to all kinds of noble work. They regarded engaging in a particular trade or line of work as also answering the call of God. The only way society can function in a civilized manner is for every person to fulfill their role in life. They taught that occupational roles are ordained by God, who calls people to do them just as He calls others to the work of ministry.

Further, they interpreted the passage, "Let every man abide in the same calling wherein he was called" (1 Corinthians 7:20 KJV), to mean Christians should seek to be contented in their occupational role. In this passage, "abide in the same calling" refers to vocational calling, while "in which he was called" refers to the gospel call. If a person is called to be a shoe cobbler or miller or farmer, they should seek to be content with their role in life and not seek other vocational employment.

Accordingly, the Puritans admonished people to always give their best in their work and emphasized that one's work should bring glory to God. They went so far as to discourage Christians from attempting to rise above their lot in life. If one's trade was a shoe cobbler, then the Christian should seek contentment with being a shoe cobbler.

Stewardship of Personal Gifts and Talents

Several of these New Testament principles about vocational calling are found in the Old Testament. When the Lord gave instructions to Moses about how to build the Tabernacle, He also identified outstanding Israelite craftsmen to do the work. Bezalel and Oholiab were appointed to design the tent, its furnishings, and the clothing for the priests. The Lord had gifted these men with the skill of understanding design, weaving fabrics, making garments, and working with woods and metals. (See Exodus 31:1–11.)

Later, when Solomon built the Temple, he imported craftsmen from Tyre to oversee its construction. These men were recruited because of their architectural and building skills. Our work should glorify God. At the end of the day, when our work is done, we should be able to say with our Creator, "It is good." Exceptional craftsmanship in our work honors our Creator. That should be the goal of our work.

The Blessings of Giving

Associated with our responsibilities to this earth is the stewardship of our talents. Jesus taught us that not only should our work bring glory to our Creator but that we should be generous and bless our neighbors with our gifts. He taught, "It is more blessed to give than to receive" (Acts 20:35 NIV). We are not designed to be reservoirs keeping all of God's blessing for ourselves but channels through which His grace can flow to bless others.

Several stories in Jesus's life illustrate how we should be generous with our love and resources. One of those stories is the Good Samaritan. A man was waylaid on his way to Jericho and left on the roadside. A Levite and priest (religious leaders among the Jews) passed by and left him lying injured on the roadside. However, a Samaritan stopped to help the injured man and used his resources to care for him. The Samaritans were despised by the Jews. However, it was a Samaritan who came to the aid of this Jewish man by using his time, money, and resources to help a person in trouble. (See Luke 10:25.)

On another occasion, Jesus taught us that if we do not use our talents, we may lose them. He told the story of three men who were given varying amounts of talents and assigned the responsibilities of taking care of these resources while their master was away on a trip. (See Matthew 25:15–28.)

Two of the three men sought to increase their master's wealth, while the third man simply buried his resources and waited for his master to return. Upon his return, the master rewarded the first two with praise, affirmation, and increased assignments. However, he took from the third servant even the small amount that he had been given and gave it to the first servant.

This parable teaches that those who faithfully use their talents to bless others are blessed and increased with more gifts and responsibilities, while those who refuse to use their talents to help others lose the ones they have.

The Matter of Ownership

These stories are also related to the principle of ownership. When God gave the Israelites the land of Palestine for an inheritance, each tribal family was instructed to be stewards of their inheritance. While they enjoyed their inheritance, they were responsible for holding it in trust for future generations. Accordingly, they were instructed to give their fields regular Sabbath rests and allow them to rejuvenate and provide food for the poor and animals. This reminded the Israelites that it is God who is the supreme owner and cares about all His creation. (See Leviticus 23:30.)

Later in Israel's history, when one of Israel's kings attempted to seize his neighbor's vineyard for his garden, the landowner refused to sell him the property. The landowner cited his responsibility for keeping his land in trust for the future generations of his posterity. (See 1 Kings 21:1.) He viewed ownership as something given to him requiring the responsibility of stewardship.

Os Guinness has traced the various attitudes of property ownership through three cultures: Greek, Roman, and Judeo-Christian. In the Greek world, the attitude toward property ownership, held by a minority of influential Greeks, was that property was owned by the community and ought to be shared by the community.

However, the Romans came along and adopted an opposite view, with owners having absolute rights. They could do whatever they wished with their property. If they chose to burn down their barn, it was no one's business but theirs.

Guinness points out that in contrast to these two opposing views, there is a third view—the Judeo-Christian view. This view teaches that God ultimately owns everything and we are simply entrusted as stewards of our property and possessions. It has been given to us by God, and we are responsible to Him for what we do with our possession (Guiness 2001).

God Uses Industrious People

A third principle is that God uses industrious people to accomplish His work. Adam was kept busy in the garden. Throughout the scriptures, it was industrious people that God used to accomplish his purposes. Moses was taking care of sheep when God called him to lead the Israelites out of Egyptian bondage. Saul was searching for his father's lost donkeys when God called him to become Israel's first king. Peter, Andrew, James, and John were working in their fishing business when Jesus called them to follow Him.

In the book of Proverbs, diligence and work are applauded as a blessing to individuals, their families, and society in general. The proverb writer calls attention to the industrious nature of the ant (see Proverbs 6:6.) and goes on to teach that poverty will come to you if you sleep when you should be working. (See Proverbs 6:9–10.) In another proverb, he teaches that laziness will cause you to go hungry. (See Proverbs 19:15.)

I once had a foreman say, "If you have a job that needs to get done, don't look for someone who doesn't have anything to do to get it done. Nine times out of ten, that person will never get the job done. Instead, find someone who has more work to do than they have time to do it, and nine times out ten, they will get the job done."

Laziness is an affront to God. In the early days of the church, the folk gave generously of their resources to care for one another. They pooled their resources to help the downtrodden, the sick, and the widows among them. However, some began adopting the attitude that they did not need to work and could live off the generosity of other Christians.

Paul straightforwardly dealt with this error in one of his early letters to the believers in the Thessalonian Church: "If a man will not work, then he shall not eat" (2 Thessalonians 3:10 NIV). Later, he emphasized this point again when he wrote to Timothy, "If anyone does not provide for his relatives, and especially for his immediate family, he has denied the faith and is worse than an unbeliever" (1 Timothy 5:8 NIV).

In the process of selecting church leaders, Paul instructed both Timothy and Titus to choose men who provided for their families. If a person fails to provide for his family, he is unqualified for church leadership. I once heard a college president remark that God cannot use lazy preachers to get His work done. In addition to not taking responsibility for their families, lazy preachers do not take responsibility for the Lord's work. He said, "If you can't preach and pay your bills, then pay your bills." In other words, your first responsibility is to provide for your family.

This principle does not nullify the call for compassionate ministries and the Christian mandate to minister to the downtrodden and those who have fallen on hard times. James teaches the very core of religious worship is caring for the orphans and widows. (See James 1:27.) One of the first orders of business in organizing the leadership of the young church was to appoint deacons to oversee its compassionate ministries. (See Acts 6:5.) As Christians, we are called to be compassionate to the downtrodden and those who have fallen on hard times. At the same time, we must guard against condoning laziness and encourage folk to take responsibility for their lives and provide for their families.

The Christian Attitude toward Work

To a greater or lesser extent, everyone should recognize God's calling in their vocational work. Accordingly, our work should be done enthusiastically and offered up to God as a sacrifice of praise. The word *enthusiasm* is a transliteration of the compound Greek word *enthusismos*. This Greek word is made up of the preposition *en*, which means "in," and *theos*, which means "god." Thus, it means "God in us." God calls for us to go about our work with enthusiasm.

Richard Bolles, who began his career as a clergyman and later transitioned into a career counselor and best-selling author, taught that we should view our work as being done before our Creator. In the epilogue to his 2014 edition of his best-selling book, *What Color Is Your Parachute*, he discusses the connection between our mission in life and our vocational calling under the heading, *What is your mission in life?* In that epilogue, he wrote:

> Our first mission in life is to seek to stand hour by hour in the conscious presence of God, the One from whom your Mission is derived ...

> Our second mission is to ... do what you can, moment by moment, day by day, step by step, to make this world a better place, following the leading and guidance of God's Spirit within you and around you ...

> Our third mission is to ...

> a) exercise that Talent which you particularly came to Earth to use – your greatest gift, which you most delight to use,

> b) in the place(s) or setting(s) which God has caused to appeal to you the most,

> c) and for those purposes which God most needs to have done in the world.

> He concludes that we share the first two responsibilities with all other members of humanity. However, the third responsibility is the one that is uniquely ours. (Bolles 1999)

In the next chapter, we examine the *Christian calling*. This is the call that engages every Christian in the Lord's work. As we will see, when all four elements of callings have been defined, they overlap and are interrelated.

Questions for Thought and Reflection

1. What is the vocational call?
2. Where did the vocational call originate?
3. When was it first given?
4. What do you think is involved in the mandate to subdue the earth?
5. What is the origin and meaning of the word *vocation*?
6. What does our stewardship of the earth involve?
7. Do you believe the righteous choices of parents bless future generations?
8. How do the sinful choices of parents negatively affect future generations?
9. What should be the Christian's attitude toward work?
10. How do you think we will be involved in work on the new earth when our redemption is complete?

Bolles, R. 1999. *What Color Is Your Parachute.* Berkley CA: Ten Speed Press.

Bookless, D. 2008. *Planet Wise.* Downers Grove: IVP.

Buechner, F. 1973. *Wishful Thinking: The Seeker's ABCs.* New York: Harper.

Dallas Willard. 2010. *A Place for Truth.* Downers Grove, IL: InterVarsity Press.

Ford, L. 1991. *Transforming Leadership Jesus' Way of Creating Vision, Shaping Values & Empowering Change.* Downers Grove, IL: InterVarsity Press.

Guiness, O. 2001. *Doing Well and Doing Good.* Colorado Springs, Colorado: NavPress.

Guinness, O. 1998. *The Call.* Nashville, TN: Word Publisher.

Richard Taylor. 1983. *Beacon Dictionary of Theology.* Kansas City: Beacon Hill Press of Kansas.

Stevens, J. P. 1999. *The Other Six Days.* Grand Rapids MI: William B. Eerdmans.

Stott, J. 2010. *The Radical Disciple.* Nottingham, England: InterVarsity Press.

Walton, J., Matthews, V., & Chavalas, M. 2000. *The IVP Bible Background Commentary Old Testament.* Downers Grove, IL: InteVarsity Press.

Wright, N. T. 2008. *Surprised by Hope: Rethinking Heaven, the Resurrection, and the Mission of the Church.* New York, NY: Harper Collins.

Our Christian Calling

Freely you have received, freely give.
—Matthew 10:8 NIV

Introduction

When Hurricane Katrina struck the Gulf Coast, leaving behind one of the worst disasters in American history, the federal government began working through its Federal Emergency Management Agency (FEMA), sending help to the gulf area. But FEMA, with its massive resources (and bureaucracy), was not the first one on the scene in some areas.

The day after the hurricane, a Salvation Army truck from Oklahoma pulled up to the Salvation Army slab in Biloxi, Mississippi, where its building had stood the day before Katrina struck, bringing the first shipment of food and water to the city of Biloxi. The Salvation Army is known for its compassionate ministry throughout the world.

In the 1850s, William and Catherine Booth felt called by the Lord to minister to London's poor people and founded the Salvation Army. They began evangelizing people, focusing on the poor, the homeless, the hungry, and the destitute. Because their methods were condemned by the established church, they were forced into the streets. Eventually, William Booth was permitted to set up a tent in a Quaker cemetery to hold evangelistic services.

It was from that tent revival in London's East End the Salvation Army was launched. "Thieves, prostitutes, gamblers, and drunkards were among Booth's first converts. He preached hope and salvation to multitudes of desperately poor people. He aimed to lead people to Christ and link them to a church for further spiritual guidance" (About Us, 2012).

Now, more than one hundred and sixty years later, the Salvation Army continues to minister to millions of distressed people by caring for them during times of devastation and disaster. Its ministry includes those caught up in human trafficking, those recently released from prison, the elderly, and downtrodden people. Their mission is to become the hands, feet, and voice of Jesus to broken people. Their mission illustrates one dimension of the Christian calling.

Over the centuries, when Christians and others fall on hard times or experience disaster, sickness, or some other type of hardship, the church has often led the way in responding to those needs. When the young church was just a few decades old, Christians around the Aegean Sea were sending aid to the suffering poor in the church in Jerusalem. Their generosity became an example of how Christians should respond to the needs of those who fall on hard times and need help.

Within the heart of every believer is the desire to reciprocate Christ's love by ministering to those around them. It is impossible to maintain a healthy, vibrant relationship with Christ without returning His love in service to others. This was one of the contributing factors to the early church's phenomenal growth.

Because the line separating the *special call* to ministry and the *Christian calling* is not always easily distinguishable, there are many areas of overlap between the two areas. This is illustrated by the Venn diagram at the beginning of the next chapter. In its broadest sense, the Christian calling encompasses all that it means to become a true disciple of Jesus Christ and faithfully obey His teachings. In short, it encompasses all the activities that are included under the umbrella of the expression Christian ministry as we seek to become the hands, feet, and voice of Jesus serving our broken world. As His followers, we are called to be the incarnation of Christ to our world. That means that our neighbors, friends, coworkers, and enemies should be able to see who Christ is through the way we live our lives and minister.

From the moment we believe in Christ until the day He calls us to heaven, we are called to do His work on earth. For some, this includes a special call to ministry. For others, it involves simply obeying the voice of the Lord as they live out their Christian faith.

The Breadth of Christian Calling

For our purpose, the *Christian calling* is defined as that inner prompting that urges us to live in harmony with Christ's teachings and do His work on earth. At times, it involves specific acts of service and calls us to use our time, talents, and resources to show His love to the world around us. Through our activities, we strive to make this world a better place as we seek the answer the question: "What would Jesus do?" It encompasses all that Jesus taught His followers to do.

Because this touches on all areas of life, sometimes it is a challenge to differentiate between the special call to ministry and the general call to Christian service. Even then, at times the separation seems to be artificial. At other times, the distinction is more pronounced and easily recognized. Because the boundaries in the scriptures are not always clear, some advocate doing away with the distinction of clergy altogether. They point out that in the New Testament there is no clear distinction between clergy and laity. Later, we will engage in this debate.

In essence, the Christian calling is the spectrum of activities done in the name of Christ that serves broken people. It calls every Christian to engage in Christian service on some level. At one end of the spectrum are those whom the Lord calls to dedicate their lives to vocational Christian ministry (the clergy). At the other end of the spectrum are those who seek to live out their Christian faith in their homes, communities, workplaces, and careers. They do not necessarily seek the official endorsement of the church through ordination but engage in a wide range of Christian activities, from the simple act of giving a cup of cold water to running world-wide organizations that care for people in distress.

As a result, some believe there should not be a separate class of Christians designated as clergy. All His followers should have a servant's heart. Our words, actions, and deeds should reflect what Jesus taught us to do. The people around us should see Christ who is alive within us.

At first, believers were called people of *the way* before they were called Christians. That expression was used to describe the way they lived. The people around them saw them seeking to follow the teaching of Jesus. To some extent, this caused them to be out of step with the world around them. Later, they were ridiculed by being called *little Christs*, which was shortened to *Christians*.

The Great Commission (see Matthew 28:19) calls all believers to share the Good News and evangelize the lost. We are called to share the hope that we have in Christ with those around us so that they too may believe and experience this Christian hope.

Another way to look at the Christian calling is to examine how our Christian faith is connected to our vocational work. There are many believers employed in the helping fields, such as medicine, education, counseling, and similar fields, who feel called to their work. They believe that their purpose on earth is to make this world a better place through their vocational work. These areas are related to the Christian calling. At times, this makes the Christian calling and special call hard to distinguish. As a result, Christians sometimes get confused when the call to ministry is discussed.

However, the practice of ordaining clergy goes back to the early centuries of the church and is firmly grounded in the scriptures. As a result, the church has understood the special call to ministry to be distinguished from the general calling to Christian service, although at times it is not always easy to separate the two.

To illustrate this overlap, examples are included at the end of this chapter of Christian leaders who had very successful careers in parachurch organizations without having been ordained for their work by a church, while other leaders have sought ordination. Many parachurch ministries are launched to fill a gap that is being overlooked by the church. Over time, some of these ministries have grown to have widespread influence within the organization of the church and prompted denominations to begin similar ministries. These stories illustrate how the Lord is not limited to a church organization to get His work done.

Christian Calling in the First Century

The first-century church did not have the organizational structure that we have today. Some of the titles used for church leaders in the ordination process did not exist when the New Testament was being written, which raises challenges when we attempt to anchor a particular ecclesiastical model in the scriptures. As a result, many of the models used today are only found in their embryonic form in the New Testament.

Further, it must be understood that the ecclesiastical organization of the church has been providentially shaped under the leadership of the Holy Spirit. Its current organizational structure safeguards the church against doctrinal error, heretical practices, missional drift, and false prophets and teachers.

The Work of Ministry

Following His ascension into heaven, Jesus instructed His disciples to carry out His work on earth and gave them the Great Commission: "Therefore go and make disciples of all nations, baptizing them in the name of the Father and of the Son and the Holy Spirit, and teaching them to obey everything I have commanded you. And surely I am with you always, to the very end of the age" (Matthew 28:19–20 NIV). Earlier, Jesus chose twelve disciples, which is parallel to the twelve tribes of Israel, and appointed them as apostles. They were sent on their first mission with the instructions to "Heal the sick, raise the dead, cleanse those who have leprosy, drive out demons. Freely you have received; freely give" (Matthew

10:8 NIV). With these words embedded in their hearts and minds, the apostles launched their mission.

Over the centuries, the church has sought to fulfill the Great Commission in a multitude of ways. In seeking to fulfill its mission, in effect, the church is answering the Christian calling, whether that is feeding the poor via a worldwide organization, taking care of orphans, or healing the sick through hospitals and clinics. The spectrum of activities in this area is so broad that it is impossible to come up with a definitive list of activities.

Serve or Minister

In the English language, the words *minister* and *serve* have different but related meanings. In the Greek language, they are the same word. Because *minister* is used as both a noun and a verb, it is easy to see where confusion can arise. As a noun, it is used to refer to spiritual leaders, and when used as a verb, it describes the activity of these leaders.

Throughout the Old Testament, *minister* is used almost exclusively to describe the activities of priests overseeing worship at the Tabernacle and temples. It appears sixty-two times in the NIV's translation of the Old Testament and appears as both a noun and a verb. It is the translation of the Hebrew word *sharath* and, in most cases, describes the activity of priests and their attendants as they carried out their duties in God's house.

In the New Testament, the words translated *minister, serve,* and *deacon* come from the same Greek root word. The word *deacon* is a transliteration of the Greek word *diakonos* and simply means to serve. It is derived from the word *doulos,* which is typically translated as *slave,* and means *to serve.* Thus, inherent in the word *minister* is the idea of serving. We often talk about a minister as one who serves a congregation. In their introductions, James, John, Jude, Paul, and Peter all use the word *doulos* to describe their roles in the church.

Bill Bright, the founder of Campus Crusade for Christ (now CRU), was asked what he wanted to be known as. He replied that he wanted to be remembered as the "slave of Jesus Christ" and noted that Peter, John,

James, Paul, and Jude all wrote they were the *doulos* of Jesus Christ (Bright, The Journey Home 2003).

In places where this Greek word is used as a verb, it is often translated as *minister*. Some churches limit their use of this word to the work of clergy, while others include the work of church staff, such as counselors, accountants, business managers, legal aids, and office personnel as ministers. One megachurch on its website advertised for an accounting staff position as a place where people could serve in "the ministry to which they are called."

In addition to its usage in religious contexts, *ministry* is also used in secular contexts, such as titles for government officials and their work. For example, England designates its chief political leader as its *prime minister*. Those serving under this person are also given titles such as *minister of education, minister of foreign affairs*, and so on. The idea inherent within this word is the person serves the public trust.

Because of its broad usage, it should not be surprising that confusion can arise when this word is used in the church. At times, it can be used to describe the work of clergy, while in other contexts it is used in a much broader sense. Those who work in Christian educational institutions, Christian media, compassionate ministries, and Christian social work often refer to their work as a ministry. With this broad spectrum of usage, it is challenging to differentiate between the ministry done by clergy and that done by the laity.

A Cup of Cold Water

From its inception, the church has been called to care for the sick and help the downtrodden. When the church started building its cathedrals in the third and fourth centuries, it included areas that were designated to care for the sick. From its early days, the church has led the way in building hospitals, orphanages, educational institutions, and similar institutions to serve their communities. Jesus taught that even the simple act of giving a "cup of cold water" has eternal value and will not go unnoticed by our heavenly Father. (See Matthew 10:41.)

Bring the Little Children to Me

Ministry to children is important to the Lord. Jesus both taught and demonstrated this principle by blessing the children who were brought to Him. He said that it would be better to be drowned with a millstone around our neck than to harm a little child. (See Matthew 18:6.) Over the centuries, the church has led the way in building orphanages, feeding hungry children, running adoption programs, and serving the educational needs of children. Children have a special place in Christ's kingdom.

In an article in *Christianity Today*, "Abba Changes Everything: Why Every Christian Is Called to Rescue Orphans," Russell Moore writes about his experience of adopting two Russian boys. When he and his wife first went to the orphanage in Russia to adopt their sons, they were surprised that there was so little noise. He soon learned the children had stopped crying because no one responded to their cries. After visiting with their sons for a week, when it came time for them to leave to wait for the adoption papers, Moore discovered the meaning of Abba in a fresh, new way.

As they were walking down the hallway to leave, he heard his son scream for the first time. Moore commented, "Little Maxim fell back in his crib and let out a guttural yell. It seemed he knew, maybe for the first time, that he would be heard ... I will never forget how the hairs on my arm stood up as I heard that yell. I was struck, maybe for the first time, by the force of the Abba cry passages in the New Testament" (Moore, 2010, 20).

Ministry to children must always be one of the church's priorities. Over the past centuries, this has taken place through Sunday schools, vacation Bible schools, daycares, Christian schools, backyard clubs, and a multitude of similar activities. Lay people often lead these ministries, feeling called to their work.

One of my students wrote about her calling in this way. While she was living as a single mother in the inner city, surrounded by broken people and looking forward to the day when she could escape that environment for a safer area, she received her life's calling. After she began attending church, something caught her attention—the children in her neighborhood. Sundays seemed to be the worst day of the week for them. Many of their parents had partied all night the night before and were sleeping off hangovers. The children were left unsupervised to fend for themselves. She began inviting them to go with her to church. Soon her car was filled to overflowing. The children were excited about going to church and escaping their environment for a few hours.

Then she noticed something else—they were hungry. Their parents were in no condition to prepare food for them. After church, she took them by McDonald's to get them a hamburger. For many, that was the only food they got that day.

Eventually, she was able to move to the suburbs. As she wrote about her calling, she commented that she could not get the children out of her mind. She wrote, "Who is looking out for the children?" and followed with a comment that I cannot forget, "If Jesus were to come to our city on Sunday morning, I don't think we would find Him in any of our fine churches. I think we would find Him on the streets with the children." I believe she is right. That seems to be the way He lived while on earth.

The Christian calling involves following the heart of Jesus to serve the people He loved. Ministry to children is very important! While there are some children's leaders who are ordained for their work, most people who work in children's ministry do not seek any type of ministerial license. They simply minister out of their love for Christ and the children He loves.

Heal the Sick

On their first mission, Jesus instructed the apostles to "heal the sick." He said, "Freely you have received; freely give" (Matthew 10:7–8 NIV). From the beginning, the church has understood the ministry of healing the sick to be an integral part of its calling. One of the first miracles of the young church under the leadership of Peter and John was healing a lame man. In those early decades, healing was understood to be an integral part of their mission and a sign that God was with them.

Very early on, the church began caring for the sick and nursing them back to health. Soon after Emperor Constantine freed Christians from government persecution and oppression, they began building hospitals. "The first ecumenical council of the Christian church at Nicaea in 325 directed bishops to establish a hospice in every city ... The first hospital was built by St. Basil in Caesarea in Cappadocia about 369 A.D" (Schmidt 2004). By the middle of the second millennium, there were an estimated 37,000 monasteries that cared for the sick. Jesus's directive to heal the sick inspired the founding of these hospitals.

Our nation is filled with hospitals that bear a founding Christian mission, such as Good Samaritan, Deaconess, Bethesda, Christ, Mercy, and so on. All these names testify to the Christian influence behind the establishment of these health care institutions. It is Christ's love that inspired these founders to establish their institutions.

Many working in the medical profession testify to being called to their work. Others have left family and friends to go as medical missionaries to remote parts of the world to care for those who desperately need medical help.

A few years ago, I was part of a team that went on a short missionary trip to the Amazon jungle. The church in that part of the jungle was experiencing phenomenal growth. In the early years, a pioneer missionary had built the first medical clinic in that region of the jungle that provided the only health care available for hundreds of miles around. His successor, a physician, brought the blessings of modern medical science to the heart of the jungle.

As a result of their Christian compassion and medical skills, many turned to Christ. It was the love of Christ that motivated these missionaries to leave behind their family, friends, and the comforts of their homeland to minister to people in the jungle.

The Breadth of the Christian Calling

Of all that can be discussed under the broad area of the Christian calling, only a few areas have been briefly mentioned. This is not even the tip of the iceberg. Volumes could be devoted to this topic alone. However, these examples illustrate how broad the spectrum of the Christian calling is. In essence, Jesus taught us that we are to love our neighbors as ourselves and further defined our neighbors as our fellow human beings.

Questions have been raised about whether the primary emphasis of the church should be its focus on social outreach through medicine and similar activities or on evangelistic activity. The truth is that one cannot take place without the other. They are interconnected and interdependent. We cannot effectively evangelize people without loving them through our activities. Neither can we fully love them without sharing the good news of Jesus Christ. We must allow the Spirit to guide us as we seek to balance these two areas.

Billy Graham wrote, "The cup of cold water comes after and sometimes before rather than instead of the gospel. Christians, above all others, should be concerned with societal problems and social injustices. Down through the centuries, the church has contributed more than any other single agency in lifting social standards to new heights" (Graham, 1984). We now turn to the clergy-laity debate.

Clergy-Laity Debate

As pointed out earlier, there was a limited ecclesiastical organization within the church in the first century compared to today. Before the third century, there were no church buildings, no ordained clergy as such, and no denominations as we have them today.

Initially, Christians sought to worship in synagogues with Jews but were soon forced out and turned to meet in one another's homes. Typically, a person of means with a large enough space to accommodate a large group of people hosted church meetings. In that environment, the need to formally ordain designated leaders was not necessary like it is today. However, as time went on, with the growth of the church and its acquisition of property, the need arose to officially designate leaders to oversee the organized church.

As a result, today, one very important administrative responsibility the church has is the ordination of its leaders. Seeking to anchor a particular model of church organization in the scriptures brings challenges. How should clergy leaders be selected? Paul includes a list of criteria for church leaders in letters to both Titus and Timothy and includes in his lists both qualifications for elders and deacons. However, his list does not include specific guidelines for women leaders, although it is easy to examine the underlying principles of those qualifications and extend them to women.

He does not specify how the ordination process is to take place, although some have suggested that the laying on of hands was an ordination ceremony. This seems to be the case with the seven deacons who were chosen to oversee this distribution of food in Acts. (See Acts 6:6.) It also appears to be the case when Paul chose Timothy as his understudy (see 1 Timothy 4:14), although, in Luke's account of Timothy's induction into the ministry, he mentions only a circumcision ritual. (See Acts 16:3.) The failure to mention any specific kind of ceremony probably indicates the situation in the early church was pretty fluid, with the leaders relying on the leadership of Spirit and the precedents of synagogues in the area.

Another question that comes to mind is whether Luke was considered a member of the clergy. Luke wrote more of the text in the New Testament than any other person. How was he regarded by the church? Was he considered clergy or not?

Clement of Rome was the first to make a distinction between church leaders and nonleaders by using the word *laity* (Barna 2002). About one hundred years later, Tertullian used the term *clergy* as a designation for church leaders. The early usage of these titles provides some foundation for the current ordination practices.

While the distinction of laity and clergy did not exist while the New Testament was being written, in and of itself, this does not forbid its usage. A little over a millennium later, Martin Luther, who led the Protestant Reformation, observed that lay Christians had equal access to Christ as did the clergy. He did not like for a spiritual distinction to be made between laity and clergy, and sought to elevate the status of the laity by teaching that all Christians are part of the priesthood of believers.

It appears the Spirit has given a certain degree of freedom to the church in how it goes about organizing its leadership and honoring those practices. The point here is not to debate this issue but to merely outline how we got to where we are today.

While ordination is the typical path to leadership in the church, God is not limited to this process. Some Christian leaders have forged careers in ministry without ordination through parachurch ministries. They, too, have felt called by the Lord to their work.

Additionally, the Christian calling has been understood by some Christians to extend into their secular work and professional lives. Some

Christian businessmen recognize that the Lord has called them to establish and run their businesses according to Christian principles. They seek to honor the Lord through their work and operate their businesses in a manner that glorifies Christ. As the Lord blesses them, many have given generously to support the work of building the Lord's kingdom.

At times, it is challenging to separate the Christian calling from and the special call to ministry. To illustrate this challenge, the stories of four men who founded and led parachurch ministries are included below. All were called by the Lord to their work. Only one of them was ordained.

Parachurch Ministries

The word *parachurch* is a word that has recently come into usage as a compound word that combines the Greek preposition *para* with the English word *church*. The Greek preposition *para* means *beside* or *alongside*. Thus, a parachurch ministry is a Christian ministry that works alongside the church with a mission that focuses on a specific need in the church.

These organizations began to emerge a couple centuries ago, at first as missionary organizations, although not referred to as parachurch organizations when they began. In the eighteenth, nineteenth, and twentieth centuries, many of these ministries began outside the oversight of denominations. However, from their inception, they worked closely alongside organized churches to carry out their mission of taking the gospel to areas of the world that did not have the Christian message.

Many of the early missionaries in these ministries did not seek ordination. However, as the missionary movement gained momentum and denominations increasingly began to embrace the idea of missionary work, they began establishing missionary departments. Today, most denominations consider missionary work to be an integral part of their ministry.

Toward the end of the nineteenth century, other Christian enterprises began to emerge, such as Christian publishing. In the twentieth century, Christian radio stations, Christian TV networks, and other similar Christian enterprises began to appear. Toward the middle of the twentieth century, evangelistic organizations such as the Billy Graham Evangelistic Organization, Youth for Christ, Campus Crusade for Christ, Focus on the

Family, and many other similar organizations emerged to work alongside the church to help round out the church's mission in its efforts to fulfill the Great Commission.

The leaders of these organizations were guided by a vision to serve a particular area of need within the church. Many of them felt called to their ministry like those who sought ordination. This is one of the reasons why it is sometimes difficult to distinguish between the special call of God that leads to ordination and the Christian calling to service.

Brother Andrew

One of these leaders was a missionary who referred to himself as Brother Andrew. He began a ministry of smuggling Bibles to Christians behind the Iron Curtain. Later, after the Berlin wall came down, he smuggled Bibles to Christians in China. He tells the story of his calling in his book, *Brother Andrew*. He enrolled in Bible school, hoping to someday become a missionary. However, because of severe back problems, he realized that no mission board would consider him for service.

Near the end of his Bible school days, he happened to see an ad in a magazine that showed impassioned young people marching in the streets of Prague, Warsaw, and Peking. It piqued his curiosity to the point that he decided to visit a youth rally in Warsaw. He wrote, "God used that magazine to lead me to a place I had never thought of going, to a suffering church that I didn't even know existed. I went to that rally as a representative of Jesus, and afterward, my life was never the same" (Becker 1996).

He continued, "Until I made that first trip to the Socialist Youth rally in 1955, I didn't have a specific plan for my life. I had never heard of Bible smuggling. At that point, all I knew was that I wanted to be a missionary ... Once I'd taken that trip, there was no turning back. From that point on I planned my life in the direction of serving the suffering church" (Becker, 1996).

He continues, "It's not about sitting around and waiting until you are absolutely certain God is calling you to a particular task, direction, country, or ministry. Nor is it waiting for the doors to open so you can go there easily. Planning is an act of faith" (Becker, 1996).

Later, Brother Andrew wrote, "God calls all of us to full-time Christian service—that is, we are all called to be Christians full time. We may not pastor a church or go to Outer Mongolia, but in God's eyes, we are just as much a part of the Great Commission as pastors and missionaries. The real calling of God is not to a certain place or career, but to everyday obedience. And that call is extended to every Christian, not a select few" (Becker, 1996).

Bill Bright

Another parachurch leader was Bill Bright. He and his wife founded Campus Crusade for Christ, now called CRU. They began their ministry while Bill was in seminary studying for the ministry. Because the organization grew so quickly, he was unable to finish his seminary degree and meet ordination requirements.

In his autobiography, Bright shares how he received the vision that launched this ministry. Late one night, while he was studying for a Hebrew exam with a friend he wrote about what happened:

> Suddenly, God in an unusual way opened my mind, touched my heart … I can't translate into English or any other language what happened but God met with me …
>
> My experience that midnight hour was so rich, so meaningful, and yet so indescribable. People have asked me what happened. There is no way I can describe it. Without apology, all I can say is I met with God. I didn't see a physical form, I didn't hear an audible voice but I have never been the same since that unforgettable encounter. (Richardson 2000)

After that experience, Bright met with his professor, who encouraged him to go forward with his vision and suggested a name for the ministry. He and his wife organized around-the-clock prayer and launched their ministry. Toward the end of his career, he reflected on the absence of a seminary degree and ordination and concluded that he was a layman and not a clergyman.

James Dobson

Another leader with worldwide influence is Focus on the Family founder James Dobson. He grew up in a minister's home and pursued a career in medicine. In college, he said he "got nervous when his cousin H.B. London answered the call to pastoral ministry. Dobson never heard that call" (Zoba, 1999). After his medical career was established, he was drawn to the area of child-rearing.

He began hosting a radio program and wrote a best-selling book, *Dare to Discipline.* His radio ministry grew to the point where he needed to resign his position at the medical school to devote his full time to the ministry. Eventually, his ministry grew to national and international influence, ministering to millions of people. In an interview with *US News and World Report,* he said, "I really do feel the prophetic role is part of what God gave me to do" (Gerson, Michael J., Major Garrett, Carolyn Kleiner, 1998). God's providence opened the doors of opportunity for Dobson to pursue his passion for the family and rearing children. In the end, he became a leading voice for the family.

Billy Graham

Perhaps the most well-known parachurch leader of all was Billy Graham. In his teens, Graham sensed a call to preach and enrolled in Bible college. There he practiced preaching away from people in a swamp near his college. Eventually, he finished college and began pastoring a church and was ordained. He went on to serve as the president of a Bible college.

Later, he was led to organize a tent crusade in the Los Angeles area. This tent meeting went on considerably longer than he planned and gained national attention. At that point, Graham realized the Lord was leading him into this type of evangelistic ministry and began organizing crusades in other cities. Eventually, he took his crusades abroad and preached to millions of people and witnessed hundreds of thousands making decisions for Christ. Of the four leaders mentioned above, only Graham was ordained.

Neither Brother Andrew, Bill Bright, James Dobson, nor Billy Graham had a model to follow when they launched their ministries. They only knew to follow God's call and allow Him to direct their paths. They walked through the doors of opportunity that opened for them. Eventually, their ministries grew beyond anything they could have imagined. Throughout his career, Brother Andrew carried millions of Bibles to persecuted Christians in restricted areas. When Bright retired, Campus Crusade for Christ had 2,600 employees and work in 160 countries. They had witnessed to millions of young people and produced the *JESUS* film that won ten million converts to Christ (Richardson 2000). Dobson had an international influence promoting family and child-rearing. Graham evangelized millions of people and preached to more people than any other person on earth.

These stories illustrate how imprecise the line is between those who are called to seek ordination and those who are called to launch innovative ministries. The Lord calls both. Both could be defined as the special call of God and illustrate how significant ministry takes place both within as well as without the organized church.

Conclusion

The Christian calling encompasses a broad spectrum of activities and calls every Christian to engage in Christian activity. Ministry begins with the simplest acts that are motivated by Christ's love, such as giving a cup of cold water, and extends to worldwide ministries. There are times when the Lord leads a person to seek ordination. However, there are other times when God calls people to dedicate their lives to a particular cause that ends up defining their careers. Only God can see the future and knows the possibilities of our ministry. We will now look at the special call of God.

Questions for Thought and Reflection

1. What challenges are involved when an attempt is made to define Christian ministry?
2. In the New Testament, what is the connection between the words *ministry*, *serve*, and *deacon*?

3. When did Christians begin building church buildings?
4. When did hospitals first appear?
5. Why is ordination, as understood and practiced in churches today, not fully described in the New Testament?
6. Read Paul's list of qualifications for church leaders in his letters to Titus and Timothy (1 Timothy 3:2–13; Titus 1:5–9). In your opinion, why did Paul include these qualifications in his list?
7. Define a parachurch ministry.
8. What new types of ministries do you envision emerging within Christianity in the twenty-first century?
9. List some of the needs that exist in the world today the church is overlooking.

Barna, F. V. 2002. *Pagan Christianity.* Carol Stream: Tyndale House/BarnaBooks.

Becker, V. 1996. *The Calling.* Moorings: Nashville.

Bright, B. 2003. *The Journey Home.* Nashville: Thomas Nelson Publishers.

Graham, B. 1984. *Peace With God.* Waco: Word Books.

Moore, R. 2010. *Christianity Today,* p. 20.

Richardson, M. 2000. *Amazing Faith.* Colorado Springs: WaterBrook Press.

Schmidt, A. J. 2004. *How Christianity Changed The World.* Grand Rapids: Zondervan.

The Special Call
(The Ecclesiastical Calling)

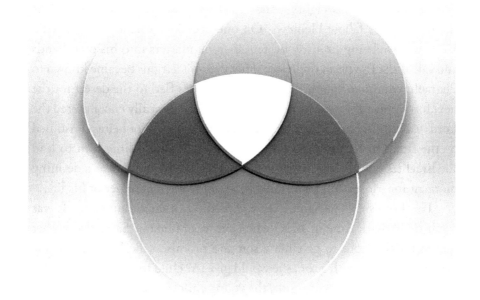

How can they call on the one they have not believed in ...
how can anyone preach unless they are sent?
—Romans 10:14–15 (NIV)

Introduction

Having briefly examined the broad spectrum of the Christian calling, we
now turn to the special call of God that leads a person to seek ordination and
devote their career to ministry. Our goal is to help the reader distinguish
between the Christian calling given to every believer and the special call
given to those who seek ordination.

The call to ministry may come in childhood, in youth, in midlife, or in some instances later in life. There are times when a person attempts to ignore God's call and pursue another career, hoping the call will go away, only to be awakened later to discover they are on the wrong career path in life. Sometimes, this happens because of a major upheaval in their lives: a job loss, an accident, a setback at work, a series of events in life that threatens their future, or some other disruption in life.

Moses was called to become the leader of the Israelites in a dramatic fashion when he was eighty years old! Earlier in life, he recognized he should help his fellow Hebrews. On one occasion, when he witnessed a Hebrew slave being unjustly beaten, he took matters into his own hands and killed the Egyptian oppressor. However, his actions became known to Pharaoh, who then sought to kill Moses. Moses fled to the desert for the next forty years. Forty years later, one day he dramatically encountered the Lord in a burning bush. The bush was on fire but was not being consumed by the fire. On that occasion, God spoke to Moses, calling him to lead the Israelites out of their bondage to the Promised Land. It was a defining moment for Moses and provided direction for the remainder of his life.

The Lord's call to Samuel also came in a dramatic moment. It was a spiritually dark time in Israel when sin was rampant. Samuel's mother prayed for the Lord to give her a son and promised the Lord that if she became pregnant with a son, she would give the child for the Lord's service for the rest of his life. As a result, the young child Samuel was born. When he was old enough to serve in the priests' courts, she left him in the care of Eli, the high priest, to serve in the Tabernacle. Sometime later during the night, he heard the Lord speaking to him. The Lord told him about the tragedy that was awaiting Eli and his sons. It was this dramatic encounter with the Lord that night that set him apart for ministry for the remainder of his life.

The Special Call

The *special call* of God refers to a call that comes from the Lord and sets a person apart for vocational ministry. Other terms that could be used are the call to full-time Christian service, the call to full-time ministry, the call to vocational ministry, the call to be a pastor, the call to be a preacher, or evangelist, or missionary, and other similar expressions. However, the expression the *special call* is used to emphasize that it is God who is calling the person to dedicate their lives to the work of ministry, and this call is recognized by the church.

While this expression is not found in the Bible, it is useful to note the comparison between the general *Christian calling* that is given to every believer and the *special calling* of God that leads a person to dedicate their lives to ministry in the church. Because *call* and *calling* have such a broad range of usage, it becomes necessary to distinguish between their various usages when discussing the ministry of a layperson versus that of an ordained minister.

These two expressions, the general *Christian calling* and the *special call* of God, parallel two terms used in theology to describe revelation: *general revelation* and *special revelation*. *General revelation* refers to how God reveals Himself to the world through creation. We can learn many things about our Creator by just looking at nature. On the other hand, *special revelation* refers to how God has specifically revealed Himself to humans primarily through the scriptures and in special appearances to His servants.

An example of general revelation is the psalmist David reveling in God's glory in creation by gazing into the heavens and marveling at the fingerprints of God's creative handiwork. He wrote, "The heavens declare the glory of God; the skies proclaim the work of his hands. Day after day they pour forth speech; night after night they reveal knowledge (Psalm 19:1–2 NIV). We can learn many things about our Creator simply by observing creation.

On the other hand, *special revelation* describes how God has specially revealed Himself to humans by speaking directly to his servants. Those encounters have been recorded in the scriptures. God appeared to Abraham and told him to relocate from Mesopotamia to Canaan and later appeared promising him offspring. Later, He appeared to Jacob and changed his name to Israel. With each appearance, God progressively revealed more about His plan of redemption for humanity.

The Lord appeared to Moses in the desert and later on Mount Sinai in dramatic fashion, giving humanity the Decalogue. The Ten Commandments were not intended to be limited to the Israelites but were given to the entire world. Following his appearance to Moses on Sinai, the Lord continued to speak to the humans through the prophets. Each new encounter with God unfolded in greater measure His revelation about His plan of redemption. It culminated with the perfect revelation in Jesus Christ. When Philip asked Jesus to show him the Father, Jesus's answer was "Anyone who has seen me has seen the Father" (John 14:8–9 NIV). Each revelation from God progressively unfolded more of God's plan of redemption for humanity.

Along the same line as the doctrine of revelation, the *special call* is used to refer to the call to vocational ministry, while the phrase the *Christian call* is used to describe the general call given to all Christians. While this analogy is not perfect, it provides a way to discuss the topic. The phrase *full-time Christian ministry* is not used because there are many bivocational pastors, tent-making missionaries, and others who feel called to their ministries and have sought ordination with their denomination.

While in more recent times the word *clergy* appears to have declined in usage, it is frequently used in this context to refer to ordained ministers. Clergy are the ones who lead congregations as pastors, missionaries, evangelists, administrative duties, and so on. They lead the ceremonial functions of the church, such as marriages, funerals, communion services, and similar activities. Because of its wide range of meaning and usage both as a noun and as a verb, *minister* is not used as often in this book.

The Ministry of Clergy and Laity Overlap

As noted in the previous chapter and illustrated by the Venn diagram at the beginning of the chapter, there are many areas of overlap between the work of clergy and that of Christians in general. Confusion often arises when we attempt to force a distinction between the work of clergy and that of Christians in general. In seeking to differentiate between the two areas, we must be careful not to overlook the fact that laypeople are sometimes as much engaged in ministry as clergy. This group includes the clergy person's spouse, many children's workers, and Christian teachers. Additionally, when the scriptures are examined to find a distinction between the two areas, it does not readily appear in the New Testament.

John's Story

John has dedicated most of his life to a career in ministry as an ordained minister, serving several churches as their lead pastor. In retirement, he has also led mission teams to third-world countries to educate pastors, build orphanages, and strengthen the church. Also, he has organized and led ministry teams to disaster areas, bringing medical and emergency supplies to help people clean up after a natural disaster. One day, I asked him to tell me about his call to ministry.

He shared that his call came after a series of tragic events in his life including the death of his daughter. She died the day after his grandfather died. A couple of years before, his father had been tragically killed in an automobile accident. All these tragedies caused him to turn to the Lord for help.

One night after the death of his daughter, he had a dream. In his dream, he had died and was standing before the Lord to give an account of his life. Standing beside him was one of his classmates from high school. As they were waiting in line to give an account of their lives, she looked over to him and asked, "Did you know this was coming?"

When he answered that indeed he knew this was coming, she then asked, "Why didn't you tell me?"

John said, "I could not get away from that dream."

It was not long after that dream that he returned to college and began preparing for the ministry. Is the story of John's call unique? Do other ministers have similar stories?

New Testament Titles

Titles that are used for church leaders in the New Testament include apostle, bishop, elder, overseer, deacon, evangelist, prophet, pastor, and teacher. Where did these titles come from and how were they used?

In the New Testament, Herod's Temple, located in Jerusalem, was the religious center of Judaism. Jewish leadership was closely associated with the Temple and included the Jewish supreme religious council— the Sanhedrin. Members of this council included the chief priest, fellow priests, leading teachers, and select Sadducees and Pharisees. Besides, there were many priests, rabbis, religious lawyers, and scribes living in the vicinity of Jerusalem who were not members of the Sanhedrin but were considered religious leaders. Many of these people would have been considered clergy by today's standards.

In addition to Herod's Temple, there were synagogues throughout Palestine where Jewish religious activities took place. It has been estimated that in New Testament times there were more than four hundred synagogues in the vicinity of Jerusalem alone. Synagogues had leaders and, if they were large enough, assistants. Some of the synagogues had rabbis associated with them. Paul's practice on his missionary journeys was to first go to the local synagogue when he first entered a new town or city. Thus, it was only natural for the early church to follow the practices of synagogues when selecting leaders.

While Jesus was on earth, he appointed twelve men as apostles, and one of them betrayed Him then committed suicide. After His ascension, the remaining eleven selected Mattathias to fill Judas's place. Soon after, when the church was growing rapidly in Jerusalem and needed leaders to oversee its compassionate ministry, deacons were chosen to administer the church's compassionate work. Stephen, the first Christian martyr, was one of the seven men chosen for this work.

When Paul and Barnabas went into Asia Minor on their first missionary journey, they appointed elders in the churches they established. Where did they get the idea for this kind of local leadership in their churches? No doubt they looked at the way appointments were made in the synagogues and followed that model.

There are times when life seems like a series of random events. However, there are other times when the Lord's providential hand is unmistakably clear and leaves little room for doubt. We go to college and meet the person who becomes our marriage partner for life. If we had not chosen to attend that specific college, it is unlikely that we would have met that person, let alone married them.

We finish college, get our first job, and relocate to another city. It just so happens that we move in next door to a Christian couple who invites us to go to church with them. As a result of that invitation, we begin attending church and eventually come to faith in Christ. Are all these just random events? Or was God's hand of providence at work in each move and decision? We will never fully understand many of the answers to these questions on this side of eternity, but what is evident is that God's providential hand is at work in our lives, accomplishing His purposes on a higher level than we can ever realize.

That seems to be the case with the church's organization as it began to take shape in the first century. While the way it was taking place in the New Testament is not always clearly described, God was at work, leading the way for the early church to fulfill its mission.

Leadership in the New Testament

In the New Testament, except for the apostles whom the Lord himself appointed, there was not a specified ordination process for clergy leaders like we have today. In addition to the apostles, the New Testament includes bishops, overseers, elders, deacons, evangelists, pastors, prophets, and teachers. While the title of prophet is a carryover from the Old Testament, the other titles, including bishops, elders, overseers, deacons, and evangelists, were new designations, some of which were borrowed from their secular usage.

To help us understand how the *special call* is used in the New Testament, four titles of clergy leaders are examined: apostles, bishops/overseers, elders, and deacons. These titles were selected because they continue to be widely used in church organizations. A word of caution is appropriate here. John Stott points out that when examining clergy titles in the New Testament, "God has not specified the precise form which pastoral oversight should take place" (Stott, 1996).

Apostle

The word *apostle* is the title used by Jesus to designate the key leaders among his followers. Jesus's initial call to the apostles was for them to simply follow Him as disciples. It came out of the rhythm and flow of Jesus's everyday ministry. He was walking beside the Sea of Galilee when he called Peter, Andrew, James, and John to become His followers. He later invited Matthew and seven more disciples to join Him. After these men had been with Jesus for some time, following a night of prayer, He chose twelve of them to be his apostles. (See Luke 6:12.)

Judas was one of the twelve but forfeited his place among the apostles by his betrayal of Jesus and subsequent suicide. After Jesus's ascension, the remaining eleven filled the place vacated by Judas by following the Old Testament method of casting lots to discern God's will. As a result, Matthias was chosen to fill Judas's place.

Later, Saul of Tarsus was converted to Christ in a dramatic experience and emerged as a preeminent leader in the young church. Several times in his letters, he refers to himself as the "apostle to the Gentiles" (see Romans 11:8 and Galatians 2:8). Three other people are also listed as apostles in the New Testament. Luke refers to Barnabas as an apostle. (See Acts 14:14.) In his closing remarks to the Romans, Paul refers to Andronicus and Junia as apostles. (See Romans 16:7.)

However, for the most part, the church has reserved the title *apostle* for members of the original group of twelve along with Paul. Although there are a limited number of churches today that use this title for select leaders, it is not frequently applied to church leaders today.

The twelve apostles were chosen for their office by Jesus Himself. In John's Gospel, on three occasions, Jesus told the twelve, "You did not choose me but I chose you and appointed you" (John 15:16 NIV). (See also John 6:70 and John 15:19.) On those occasions, Judas is included in the list of apostles. However, Judas forfeited his place of honor through his betrayal of Jesus.

Bishop/Overseer

The second Greek word for church leaders used in the New Testament is the word *episkopos*. This word is translated as both *bishop* and *overseer*. In secular literature, this word was used in both political and military contexts to refer to a person who was assigned a superintending role (Keener 1993). In the Scriptures, this word communicates the superintending role of a pastor (Stott, Guard the Truth 1996).

It is used in both Acts and Paul's letters to refer to church leaders. In Acts, Luke used it about church leaders in Ephesus. (See Acts 20:28.)

In his first letter to Timothy, Paul wrote, "Now the overseer must be above reproach, the husband of but one wife, temperate, self-controlled, respectable, hospitable, and able to teach" (1 Timothy 3:1–2 NIV). He gives similar instructions to Titus, "Since an overseer is entrusted with God's work, he must be blameless—not overbearing, not quick-tempered, not given to drunkenness, not violent, not pursuing dishonest gain" (Titus 1:7 NIV). Peter also uses this word about Jesus being the "Shepherd and overseer of your souls" (1 Peter 2:25 NIV).

Throughout the New Testament, it is used to describe those with responsibility for the spiritual welfare of the local body of believers but does not take on the distinction that it carries today. In the second century, it began to take on the meaning of a person who oversaw several churches in a particular region. A few centuries later, this title came to refer to a person who oversaw a group of churches in a regional area. Many denominations reserve this title for higher-ranking clergy who have oversight of a group of churches in a particular region. Our English word *episcopalian* is a transliteration of this Greek word.

Elder

A third word used to describe church leaders in the New Testament is the Greek word *presbyteros,* or *elder.* Our English word *presbyterian* is a transliteration of this Greek word. It is used of an "older person" who has official leadership responsibilities in a community (Arndt and WilburGringrich 1957).

In the New Testament, the Greek words *bishop* and *elder* were used interchangeably. John Stott explains, "In New Testament times it is all but certain that *episkopos* (overseer, bishop) and *presbyteros* ('presbyter,' 'elder') were two titles for the same office" (Stott, 1996).

In Jewish communities, older men were appointed to leadership roles in their synagogues and assigned the title elder. Many of the members of the Jewish Sanhedrin were referred to as elders.

On their way back through Asia Minor while on their first missionary journey, Paul and Barnabas appointed elders as they revisited the churches they had established. (See Acts 14:23.) The church in Jerusalem is described as being under the leadership of the apostles and elders. (See Acts 15:2.) Elder was widely used in Jewish circles, and that usage was carried forward into the early church.

For example, Paul wrote to Timothy, "The elders who direct the affairs of the church well are worthy of double honor, especially those whose work is preaching and teaching ..." (1 Timothy 5:17 NIV). When Paul chose Timothy to go along with him and Silas on their second missionary journey, he sought the affirmation of the elders for the appointment of Timothy as his understudy. (See 1 Timothy 4:14.) Later, Paul instructed Titus to "appoint elders in every town" (Titus 1:5 NIV). Peter refers to himself as an elder: "I appeal as a fellow elder" (1 Peter 1:5 NIV). Thus, in the first century, *elder* was widely used as a title for local church leadership. Some denominations use that title today and designate their ordained clergy. In other church circles, this title is used to designate nonordained local leaders.

Deacon

A fourth New Testament word used for Church leaders is *diakonos* or *deacon*. Our English word is a transliteration of this Greek word and refers to one who *waits tables* or *ministers*. While Luke does not use this word to describe Stephen's role of overseeing the distribution of the church's compassionate ministries in Acts 6, it clearly describes his role. It is used later, along with overseers and elders, to describe leadership roles within local congregations.

Some denominations use the title *deacon* to refer to specialized ministries, such as compassionate ministries, educational ministries, or a similar type of ministry. They ordain people to these specialized ministries using the title *deacon*. As in the case of elder, there are some churches that use deacon to refer to local church leadership roles that do not require ordination. In these instances, elders typically have higher administrative roles than deacons.

In conclusion, the New Testament usage of titles such as apostle, bishop, overseer, elder, and deacon was developing during the first century and used in both secular and sacred environments. However, over time, they took on distinctive meanings within the church.

Priest

Another title used for clergy in some denominations, including the Roman Catholic Church, the Greek Orthodox Church, the Anglican Church, the Coptic Church, and the Lutheran Church, is the title of *priest*. This title is borrowed from the Old Testament's system of priests who oversaw worship at the Tabernacle and later temples. Their primary roles were overseeing the ceremonial practices as worshippers offered their sacrifices at the altar, inspecting people regarding health issues, and similar activities among the Israelites. In earlier times, the high priest was often brought in to discern the Lord's will by using the Urim and Thummim.

During the time of Christ, the high priest's office had become political and was controlled by Rome. However, within Judaism, the function of the priest ceased when Herod's Temple was destroyed by the Romans in AD 70. Today, Jewish congregations and synagogues are led by rabbis.

It must be kept in mind that there is one significant difference between the Old Testament priests and today's pastors. Except for Aaron, the first high priest, Old Testament priests were chosen according to birth order within their family line rather than by a special calling. Today, a pastor is expected to have a special call from God. Being born into a pastor's family is not sufficient to qualify a person to lead the church. It requires more—the call of God.

It is expected that those who seek ordination have received a call from God. This raises the question of what Paul meant when he wrote to Timothy, "Whoever aspires to be an overseer desires a noble task" (1 Timothy 3:1 NIV). John Stott comments about this verse, "It is laudable to desire this privilege". He goes on to ask, "Is not becoming a pastor a matter rather of divine call than human aspiration?" and then answers his question, "Yes, elsewhere Paul clearly affirms the call and appointment of God. So, what we call the 'selection' of candidates for the pastorate entails according to Paul three essentials: the call of God, the inner aspiration and conviction of individuals concerned, and the conscientious screening by the church as to whether they meet the requirements which the apostle now goes on to list" (Stott, *Guard the Truth* 1996). Let us take a closer look at these three criteria in the special call of the Lord.

It Is God Who Calls

Those who enter ministry must know they are called by the Lord. People do not self-select into vocational ministry. Their calling must come from the Lord, and they must know that God has spoken to them. There may be times when it takes a little time for a person to recognize the Lord is calling them. Samuel made three trips to Eli before he finally recognized it was the Lord who was speaking to him. Sometimes the Lord uses a person's situation or circumstances to direct their attention toward His calling. When a person is uncertain about whether it is the Lord's voice, the Lord is faithful to add more evidence until the person confidently knows the Lord is speaking.

Not all ministers have a dramatic moment encounter with God as did Moses and Paul. Sometimes the call happens when a person steps forward to fulfill a need in the church. One ministerial candidate shared that his call came while he was serving in a leadership role in his church as it went through a pastoral change. After several months of being without a pastor, he began filling the pulpit on Sundays. After a few months in this role, he realized that God was speaking to him about pastoring the church, and he left his insurance business to lead his church. The conviction that he should become pastor grew as he regularly filled the pulpit on Sundays, which led him to enroll in a ministry-training program and prepare for ordination.

Sometimes the call comes when a person sees a particular need in the church and recognizes they have the skills for that job. Nehemiah's call came in this manner.

There are times when the Lord uses another person, such as a church leader, to prompt a person to consider the Lord's call. This was the case with Elisha. The Lord sent Elijah to anoint Elisha as his successor. When Elijah arrived at his house, Elisha was out in the field working. However, when Elijah's mantle fell on him, the Spirit of the Lord came mightily upon him and forever changed him. (See 1 Kings 19:19–21.)

A Pastor's Story

He grew up in an alcoholic's home and could count on one hand the number of times he attended church in his childhood. When he was in elementary school, he recalls an incident when his grandmother, who was not a religious person, said to him and his older brother, "Someday one of you boys is going to be a preacher." To this day, he is puzzled by what prompted her to make that assessment.

One night when he was in middle school, his father took him and his older brother fishing. During the night, his father started the car to warm up, and the boys fell asleep in the back seat. The car's rear window was broken out, and fumes from the car's exhaust drifted into the back seat where the boys were sleeping. Toward morning, his father, who had been drinking heavily that night, sensed something was wrong and attempted to awaken the boys. Both boys were asphyxiated with carbon monoxide poisoning, and his father rushed them to the hospital. They were able to save his life, but his brother died.

In his teens, he often questioned why he was allowed to live while his brother died. During his senior year of high school, he began dating a girl whose father required them to attend church to date. For the first time in his life, he began attending church regularly. As he approached graduation, the thought occurred to him that maybe he should consider becoming a preacher. He went to his girlfriend's pastor and asked, "How can you know if you should become a preacher?"

Her pastor brushed off his question, telling him, "You're not called to be a preacher. Forget it." He did!

He graduated from college and began a successful career in business. During this period, he was very active in his church. He commented about this period of his life, "I was a pastor's ideal layman."

However, after twenty years of climbing the corporate ladder with glowing reviews, he received an evaluation that placed him lower than excellent. This was the lowest evaluation he had ever received, and he went to his supervisor to inquire about his review. His supervisor brushed off his questions and did not have a good explanation for the evaluation. He told him to forget it. His subsequent reviews were back up where they were before. However, he could not get this incident out of his mind and began to reassess his life. Not long after that incident, one evening at dinner, he asked his wife, "What would you say if I said I was going into the ministry?"

To his surprise, she replied, "If that's what you believe you should do, I will fully support you."

He continued, "When she answered me in that manner, I knew God was calling me into the ministry." Over the next months, he resigned from his position and enrolled in seminary. When his company learned of his plans to resign, they sought to keep him on as an employee by creating a special position that would allow him to attend seminary. He said, however, "I knew the Lord had called, and there was no turning back."

When I met him, he had been in ministry for over a decade. As he shared his story, he remarked at the end of our conversation, "In high school, if that pastor had encouraged me to consider the ministry, I most likely would have dedicated my entire career to ministry, not just the second half."

A Passion for Ministry

A second criterion for the call to ministry is a passion for the Lord's work. There are times when a person feels as though they do not have the abilities required to be a minister. However, they have a burning desire to serve the people of God and build His kingdom. A passion for ministry is the most important element for the special call to ministry. John Stott understands this is what Paul meant when he wrote to Timothy, "Whoever aspires to be an overseer desires a noble task" (1 Timothy 3:1 NIV).

A person may feel as though they are not qualified for the Lord's work, yet they sense the Lord pressing upon them a concern about His work. Moses felt his speech challenges disqualified him from God's calling. Jeremiah felt his youth stood in the way of God's call. Paul questioned if his prior persecution of the church prevented him from having a leading role in the church. In every instance, the Lord had already considered all their objections when He called them.

Sometimes, when God calls, He awakens within a person latent talents, interests, gifts, and abilities. Moses believed that he was not able to sufficiently communicate with Pharaoh because of his speech problem and asked the Lord to send his brother Aaron as a spokesman. However, after several encounters with Pharaoh, Moses stopped relying on Aaron to communicate the prophet's message and began delivering the messages himself. He discovered he was more qualified than he thought he was.

Blane Smith points out that initially the Lord provides more specific direction than He does later. As the person matures and gains more experience in walking with the Lord, God's leadership is often not as direct. Just as parents give their children increasing freedoms as they mature, in a similar way, the Lord entrusts a greater measure of responsibility to his faithful servants (Smith 1991). That is not to say the Lord walks away from the person. The Lord never abandons us and always faithfully guide us as we seek His direction for ministry.

The Church Affirms God's Call

A third criterion for the special call is the screening process of the church. Denominations have committees that examine candidates to determine if they are matched for ministry leadership roles. Typically, ministerial candidates are examined when they initially apply for a minister's license and observed as they progress through the candidacy period. Finally, they are examined again prior to ordination.

This third step, affirmation by the church, is not an infallible process. Church leaders can and sometimes do make mistakes. They are cautioned to carefully observe those being ordained to the Lord's work and guard against unwise choices. Paul wrote to Timothy that those who were being ordained to the ministry "Must first be tested; and then if there is nothing against them, let them serve as deacons" (1 Timothy 3:10 NIV). In the same letter, he wrote, "Do not lay hands upon anyone too hastily and thereby share responsibility for the sins of others" (1 Timothy 5:22 ASV).

I met him at a ministry-training conference. He was an ordained minister and assigned to keeping the educational records of ministers in his district as they progressed toward ordination. I asked him to share with me the story of his call.

In college, he excelled in mathematics and graduated with a degree in mathematics. Later, he came to faith in Christ, and as he grew in his newfound faith, he felt impressed that he should go into the ministry. He resigned from his job, moved his family several hundred miles away, and enrolled in seminary. Upon completion of the church's educational requirements for ordination, he returned to his home area and was given a minister's license. His first assignment was a small church in his district. Under his leadership, the small congregation grew even smaller. Soon, he resigned and moved to another small church. His experience at the second church was like his experience at the first church. He then moved to a third church, with a similar experience.

Meanwhile, to provide for his family, he took a government job as a computer engineer. With his mathematical aptitude and skills, he quickly discovered that he was gifted in computer programming. He received several promotions and enjoyed that line of work.

Eventually, he resigned from his small church to focus on his engineering career. From time to time, he was invited to fill the pulpit of small congregations and served his district as secretary of their education board. Near the end of our conversation, I asked him if he missed pastoring. He indicated that he did not. I followed with a question, if perhaps he thought that he may have misunderstood his calling. He paused a few moments to reflect on what I had just asked and commented, "I'm beginning to wonder about that myself."

How Leaders Were Chosen in the New Testament

On their first missionary journey, when Paul and Barnabas appointed elders in the churches they had established, they most likely used a selection process like that used in synagogues. They observed the leadership skills of the people in each church and selected elders from that group of men.

On his second missionary journey with Silas, when Paul arrived at Lystra, he chose Timothy as an understudy. Timothy had a good name in his area and a godly spiritual heritage in both his mother and grandmother. (See Acts 16:1–3.) Paul saw potential in Timothy and chose him to become his understudy. He called together the local leaders, had them lay their hands on him, and took him along on his second journey. (See 1 Timothy

4:14.) After Timothy's selection, Paul had him circumcised so they would not be hindered when ministering in Jewish circles. (See Acts 16:3.)

In Paul's letters to Timothy and Titus, he included a list of qualifications that was likely in the early stages of development when he selected Timothy as his understudy. The selection process for recognizing those who God calls into the ministry must follow a well-thought-out and thoroughly approved screening process. It is not sufficient for a person to merely claim the Lord has called them into the ministry. The church must verify their call.

The Ordination Process

The ordination process officially endorses and licenses leaders in the church. The word *ordain* has strong connotations within religious circles with origins in Latin, French, and English. It means "to invest with ministerial or sacerdotal functions" (Webster 1996). In the Old Testament, this word is associated with the appointment of Aaron and his sons and the line of priests in Israel.

How does this process work? Ordination typically involves three distinctive steps. The first step requires meeting the educational requirements of the sponsoring denomination. Typically, there are a minimum number of educational requirements that must be met before a person is eligible for their first ministerial license. The initial license authorizes them to practice ministry under the supervision of a board or ordained minister and works like an apprenticeship program.

Some denominations require advanced degrees such as a master of divinity degree or its equivalent for ordination. Other denominations require a bachelor's degree with a major in religious studies. Others require the completion of a specific list of courses.

The second step is an apprenticeship period where the candidate engages in ministry under the supervision of an ordained minister or board and gains experience through practicing ministry. During this period, many candidates serve as pastors of smaller congregations or work in various staff positions under a lead pastor. It is a time when many discover specific areas of ministry that match their skills and interests. This period also allows the church to observe the candidate and determine if they have the gifts and graces necessary for successful ministry.

There are a few times during this period when candidates discover they have misunderstood their calling and withdraw from the process. There are other times when ordination boards discover that the person is not suited for ministry and advise them toward another career.

The third and final step is ordination itself. This comes after the candidate has met the educational and experience requirements of their denomination. The candidate meets with an examining board that verifies that the candidate has met both the educational and practical requirements and determines that indeed the Lord has called them to the work of ministry. Upon the board's approval, there is a formal ceremony in which the person is ordained to the ministry by denominational officials.

Unlike the business model that often recruits people for leadership positions in their organizations, the church must work under the leadership of the Lord, who is the ultimate Caller. The church has the responsibility to challenge its youth to consider careers in ministry. Just as leaders often challenge youth to consider a career in medicine, or law, or education, or some other profession, the church should not overlook its responsibility of passionately challenging its youth to consider ministry as a calling.

Most denominations understand this calling to be a lifetime calling and use a passage from Romans to support this position, "For the gifts and the calling of God are irrevocable" (Romans 11:29 ESV). The only action that disqualifies a person from this calling is a significant moral failure by the minister. Even then, it does not necessarily release the person from the call. Some contend that although a minister may destroy the effectiveness of their testimony by unfaithfulness, their call is never rescinded.

Perhaps another way of answering this question is to recognize that the basic blueprint for the person is given to them at conception and continues with them throughout life. From their formation in the womb, they are given the gifts, talents, interests, and personalities that suit them for one vocation and not another. This blueprint is known by the Creator when He calls the person. These gifts typically remain with the person throughout a lifetime, unless there is a calamity such as an accident, disease, or some other event that alters or uproots these gifts.

Finally, the Lord anoints those He calls. When Saul was called to be

Israel's first king, he was anointed by Samuel for this role. He quickly experienced the Lord's anointing when he met a group of prophets and their spirit inhabited him. (See 1 Samuel 9 and 10.) He discovered the Lord's anointing enabled him to lead the Israelites. However, he tragically lost that anointing through disobedience and became ineffective as Israel's leader. (See 1 Samuel 28.)

Conclusion

At first glance, the path to ordination may be rather lengthy and involved. However, from the moment a person recognizes that God has called them to the work of ministry, they also discover that He is faithful to guide them in the path of His call. It is the special call that sets a person apart for the work of ministry. It is divine in its origin and involves recognition by the church. We now examine how that call comes in part II.

Questions for Reflection

1. Describe the special call of God.
2. How is it to be distinguished from the general Christian call?
3. What is the source of the special call?
4. What is the role of the church in that call?
5. What does the word *apostle* mean?
6. What does the word *bishop* mean?
7. What does the word *elder* mean?
8. What does the word *deacon* mean?
9. What was the function of the priests in the Bible?
10. How were priests called into their roles?
11. How are ordained ministers called into their roles as ministers?

Arndt, W., & Wilbur Gringrich, F. 1957. *A GreekIIEnglish Lexicon of the New Testament.* Chicago: The University of Chicago Press.

Keener, C. S. 1993. *The IVP Bible Background Commentary.* Downers Grove: IVP.

Smith, M. B. 1991. *Knowing God's Will.* Downers Grove, IL: InterVarsity Press.

Stott, J. 1996. *Guard the Truth.* Downers Grove: Inter-Varsity Press.

Webster. 1996. *Webster's Encyclopedic Unabridged Dictionary of the English Language.* New York: Ramdom House Value Publishing, Inc.

PART II

*Guidance for a
Fulfilling Journey*

God: The Caller of the Called

Paul, a servant of Christ Jesus, called to be an apostle and
set apart for the gospel of God.

—Romans 1:1 (NIV)

The Bible is filled with stories of people who were called to their work by
God. One of the first to be called to a special work was Noah. The Lord gave
him the task of building an ark to save his family and the animal kingdom
from an impending flood. That is followed by the call of the patriarchs and
continues throughout the Bible. It seems whenever a need arose among the
people of God in answer to their prayers for the Lord's help, God answered
their prayers by calling a leader. Those whom God called experienced a time
when God intersected their lives and gave them work to do.

The people whom God called had faults, weaknesses, frailties, and failures in their past. Many were overwhelmed by the task God was assigning them and often reasoned that He was making a mistake in calling them—He should seek someone else for the job. Nevertheless, the one who "knit us together in our mother's womb" (Psalm 139:13 AMP) knows exactly what we are made of and how He can accomplish His work through us. Furthermore, there is nothing in our past that God does not already know about when He calls us.

In the next chapter, these unique experiences are divided into three broad categories to help us understand the methods God uses when He speaks calling us to His work. They included the dramatic moment encounter with God, God sending another person to communicate His call, and awakening within us awareness about a need in His work.

The aspirational goals of many students change during their college careers. By the time they graduate, some have decided not to pursue a career in their major field of study. This also happens to those who enroll in college to study for the ministry. By the time they finish college, they have concluded that a career in ministry is not what they should pursue.

The opposite also happens. Right before graduation, I asked a business student where I would find him in ten years. I expected him to answer in a successful business career. His reply surprised me: "In ten years, most likely I will be preaching. I know that is what I should do."

Some are held back from answering the call to ministry by fear. They are afraid they will not succeed if they pursue ministry. Others conclude that they are not suited for ministry. They love the Lord and desire to serve Him but have doubts about whether they are called to be a minister.

A word of caution is needed here. Throughout scripture, many have felt they were not qualified for the work of the Lord, yet the Lord called them, and they discovered that His grace compensated for their human frailties and weaknesses. That was the case for Moses, Gideon, Jeremiah, and many others in the Bible. Many of them had latent talents that were awakened by the Lord's call, and they discovered they had gifts they did not recognize.

In the New Testament, Jesus began His ministry by calling disciples to follow Him and learn from Him. Later he chose twelve of them as His apostles. After His ascension into heaven, He gave them the gift of the sanctifying presence of the Holy Spirit. Later, He appeared to Saul on the road to Damascus and called him to be an apostle to the Gentiles and continued to work in the church by calling people into His service.

For some, His call came in a dramatic encounter as Paul experienced on the road to Damascus. For others, that call came when the Lord sent one of His servants to communicate the call, as he did with Paul and Timothy. A third method God used was to speak quietly to the person and awaken within them concern about a need in His kingdom, as He did with Barnabas. Over time, the urgency of this need grew to a level where they sensed a responsibility to do something about it. For some, it became a burning passion, as was the case with Nehemiah. The Lord often uses any one or all three of these methods when He calls a person into ministry.

In working with hundreds of young people and scores of adults who have entered the ministry, I have met very few who, in the end, misunderstood God's call. Many of their questions early on were answered as they matured in the faith and continued to walk faithfully with the Lord. Over time, they discovered that it became easier to recognize God's voice as they walked faithfully with Him.

For a period, I directed an adult education program designed for second-career adults who were preparing for the ministry. It was not uncommon to hear stories from them about not heeding God's call in their youth, only years later to be reawakened to that call. After spending several years in a spiritual wilderness, when they began to earnestly seek God's will for their lives, their call was rekindled. Sometimes it came as the result of a major upheaval in their lives.

One student shared that he grew up in a Christian home and in youth sensed the Lord calling him into the ministry. However, he resisted God's call and chose rather to go in a different direction with his career. He found a good job in an interesting field and poured his life into building a successful career. During that period of his life, he married, began raising his family, bought a nice home, and settled in to live the American dream, while not giving much attention to his relationship with Christ.

However, one day he received word that his company had been bought out by another company and his job was being phased out. Now his life was in crisis. He knew it would take several months to find another job with a comparable salary and benefits. He had a family and financial obligations. How was he going to pay the bills? What was he to do?

During this crisis, he turned to the Lord for help. As he began asking the Lord for help, he was brought once again to a call to ministry. When he finally made peace with the Lord about his call and began to prepare for the ministry, he discovered a newfound peace. Each step he took toward answering the call brought an increasing affirmation he should be in ministry.

It is important to keep in mind that it is God who calls us, and we can respond to His call or reject it. In the book of Hebrews, the author writes about the Old Testament priests, "And no one takes this honor on himself, but he receives it when called by God, just as Aaron was" (Hebrews 5:4 NIV). The origin of the special call to ministry is always God. God is sovereign and calls whom He chooses for His work.

The Call of the Patriarchs

When God began unfolding His plan of redemption to humanity, one of the first men He called was Abram. Likely, Abram was a polytheist living in the upper Euphrates Valley when he heard God's call. Living within the polytheistic influence of his family, friends, and neighbors, he would have been taught to worship a plethora of gods. It was out of this confused worship that God said to Abraham, "Go from your country, your people and your father's household to the land I will show you" (Genesis 12:1 NIV). As a result, Abraham moved to Canaan and began to worship the Lord alone who had spoken to him.

Upon his arrival in Canaan, the Lord promised him, "To your offspring, I will give this land" (Genesis 12:7 NIV). When he was ninety-nine years old, the Lord appeared again, giving him the covenant of circumcision, and promised that he would have children through his wife, Sari. On that occasion, the Lord changed his name to Abraham and Sari's name to Sarah. The next year, Isaac was born to Abraham and Sarah.

Later, God appeared to Isaac and reaffirmed the covenant he had made with his father, Abraham. (See Genesis 26:25.) Isaac continued the religious tradition of his father by building an altar to worship the Lord when he settled in Beersheba.

The Lord also appeared to Isaac's son Jacob when he was fleeing for his life from his twin brother, Esau. Because of his deceitful and conniving ways, Jacob had cheated his brother Esau out of his inheritance and blessing and was forced to flee from his home in Canaan to the upper Euphrates Valley to live with relatives. On his way to his uncle Laban's house, he encountered the Lord in a dream at Bethel. In that dream, he saw a ladder extending into heaven. (See Genesis 28:13 ff.) During this encounter, God affirmed to Jacob the covenant He had made with his grandfather, Abraham.

Once in Aram, Jacob continued his deceitful ways in his uncle Laban's house, building his wealth and family. Eventually, though, his dishonesty caught up with him, and he again was forced to flee. His father-in-law and brother-in-law became envious of his wealth and sought to retaliate against him. Jacob fled for his life back to Palestine.

Behind him were an angry father-in-law and brother-in-law. Ahead of him was an angry twin brother, Esau. During this crisis in his life, the Lord met with a repentant Jacob. (See Genesis 32:22.) Throughout the night, Jacob struggled with the Lord's angel, and when morning came, his name was changed to Israel. God reaffirmed to him the promise he had made with Abraham. His struggle with the Lord that night caused his hip joint to become out of the socket, leaving him physically changed. Jacob limped away from this experience a different man.

In their encounters with the Lord, the patriarchs did not go out to seek God. Instead, as they were in the middle of life with its challenges and responsibilities, they were met by the Lord, and their lives were forever changed.

Moses and Joshua

After enjoying years of favor with the Egyptians, the Israelites suddenly found themselves out of favor with Egypt's new rulers. The Hebrew women were ordered to throw all their newborn baby boys into the river. It was during this time that Moses was born. He was miraculously saved and spent his first forty years in the palace, his next forty years in the desert, and his final forty years leading Israel. No doubt Moses had many times to reflect on the circumstances of his birth and his days as an infant. What was his purpose in this world?

As a young man, when he witnessed an Egyptian abusing a Hebrew slave, he took matters into his hands and killed the Egyptian slave master. This action was soon discovered, and he was forced to flee to the desert for his life, where he spent the next forty years. When he was eighty years old, after spending forty years taking care of the flocks for his father-in-law, the Lord appeared to him and called him to lead the Israelites out of their Egyptian bondage to the land of their forefathers. His call is discussed in more detail in the next chapter.

Near the end of his life, the Lord instructed Moses to anoint Joshua as his successor. (See Deuteronomy 34:9.) Joshua had been Moses's special assistant on Mount Sinai while Moses received the Ten Commandments and was handpicked by Moses as the general to lead Israel's armies in their fight against the Midianites.

Upon Moses's death, the Lord appeared to Joshua and said, "As I was with Moses, so I will be with you; I will never leave you nor forsake you. Be strong and courageous, because you will lead these people to inherit the land, I swore to their ancestors to give them" (Joshua 1:5–6 NIV). The Lord confirmed His call of Joshua by miraculously causing the waters of the Jordan River to stop flowing downstream during the flood season and allowing the Israelites to cross over on a dry riverbed. (See Joshua 3:16.) Later, he helped Joshua and the Israelites take the city of Jericho without firing a shot, further confirming Joshua's leadership role over the people of Israel. (See Joshua 5:20–21.)

The Judges

Following Joshua's death, from time to time, the Israelites were led by judges who were called by the Lord. When the people drifted away from God, He allowed the neighboring people to form raiding bands and invade their land. They would cry out to the Lord in prayer, and the Lord would raise leaders who were called judges to deliver the people. Eventually, the people would drift back into their old ways, and the cycle would be repeated. This cycle continued throughout the time of the judges until the time of Samuel the prophet. Many of these judges provided much-needed spiritual leadership for the people.

One of those judges was Deborah, who served in both the roles of prophet and judge. During her time, the Israelites were being overrun by Jabin and Sisera. The Lord sent her to Barak to call him into service as the commander of the Israelites. Barak agreed to go on the condition that Deborah would accompany him into the battle. She agreed but pointed out that it would be a woman who would receive the credit for winning the day. In the end, it was a woman named Jael who killed Sisera as he fled from the battlefield. (See Judges 4:4–21.)

Another judge was Gideon. He was threshing grain in a winepress to hide his harvest from raiding hordes of Midianites when an angel appeared to him and called him into service. The angel assured Gideon that the Lord was on his side. Gideon questioned that if that was the case, why were they being overrun by the hordes of Midianites? That day, the angel said to Gideon, "Go in the strength you have and save Israel out of Midian's hand" (Judges 6:14 NIV).

Gideon began his day concerned about being robbed of his grain by the Midianites and ended his day thinking about how he would defeat the Midianites. After God's call, his first action was to destroy the idol shrine of Baal.

Next, Gideon assembled 32,000 Israelites to fight the Midianites. The Lord informed Gideon that he had too many men for the battle. Consequently, Gideon told all the men who were afraid to go home, and 22,000 men left. But the ten thousand who remained were still too many for the job.

The Lord then instructed Gideon to take his army of ten thousand down to the river and watch how they drank. He was to choose only those who drank by cupping their hands together. "Separate those who lap the water with their tongues as a dog laps from those who kneel to drink" (Judges 7:5 NIV). Those who lapped water like a dog were the ones who were vigilant and observing as to what was going on around them while they drank. The Lord instructed Gideon to take only these three hundred men for the battle.

The Lord uses those who are alert and not afraid of the battle to serve His purpose. He does not build His kingdom with lazy people. Those who are lazy in other areas of life are also unlikely to succeed in the Lord's work. That is not to say that a powerful conversion experience cannot radically change a person's motivation and transform their outlook to the point they are motivated to attempt things they never dreamed possible.

The Call of Samuel

Samuel led Israel during the transition from the judges to that of the monarchy. Samuel filled the roles of prophet, priest, and judge. He was conceived in answer to the prayer of his mother, Hannah. She asked the Lord to give her a son, and, in turn, she would dedicate him to the Lord's service for life. (See 1 Samuel 1:11.) When her son was born, she followed through with her promise, and when he was old enough to be weaned, she dedicated him to the Lord's service in the Tabernacle as an apprentice under the tutelage of the priest Eli.

As a youth just as Samuel settled into his routine in Tabernacle service, one night he heard someone calling his name. At first, he thought it was Eli and ran to him three times before Eli told him it may be the Lord speaking to him. When the Lord called a fourth time, Samuel followed Eli's instructions and responded, "Speak, LORD, for your servant is listening" (1 Samuel 3:9 NIV). That night, the Lord revealed to Samuel what He was about to do to Eli and his family because of their sin. (See 1 Samuel 3:10–14.) His encounter with the Lord that night called him into the prophet's role as a youth.

The Call of the Kings

Several decades later, Samuel was sent to Saul and later to David to anoint them as Israel's first two kings. Both Saul and David were in the routines of their lives when Samuel came to anoint them as Israel's first two kings. Saul was searching for his father's donkeys and decided to go to the prophet Samuel's house to see if he could help them locate the donkeys. He was surprised when he met Samuel and was invited to a feast the next day and given the seat of honor.

On that occasion, Samuel took Saul to the edge of town and anointed him as Israel's king. On his way home, Saul experienced a life-transforming experience when he met a group of prophets, and the Spirit of the Lord came upon him. (See 1 Samuel 4:1–13.) Three days before, he was concerned about lost donkeys. Now he was thinking about what his future looked like.

A few decades later, a similar scene played out when the Lord sent Samuel to Bethlehem to anoint David as Saul's successor. Saul failed to obey the Lord and was rejected as Israel's king. Because of his disobedience, he no longer had the Spirit's anointing and was unable to lead the nation. As a result, the Lord sent Samuel to Bethlehem to anoint David as Israel's next king. When Samuel arrived in Bethlehem, David was in the field taking care of sheep. After Jesse had called his sons to come before Samuel to discern whom the Lord had chosen, Samuel was not satisfied. Finally, David was brought in from the field. When Samuel laid eyes on him, he recognized he was looking at Israel's next king. David went on to become Israel's greatest king. David began that day thinking about taking care of sheep and ended the day thinking about what the future held for him. (See 1 Samuel 16:13.)

After David's reign, the succession of Israel and later Judah's kings followed David's family line like the way the succession of the priests was passed from one generation to the next along the line of Aaron and the Levites. Later, when the northern kingdom of Israel broke away from Judah and formed the separate kingdom of Israel, several dynasties ruled the Northern Kingdom until it was finally overthrown by the Assyrians. Each dynasty passed along the succession of leadership through its family line until the Lord sent one of His prophets to install a new dynasty. In the case of the Northern Kingdom's first king, it was a prophet from Shiloh who announced to Jeroboam that the Lord was tearing away from Judah ten of the tribes and giving them to him. (See 1 Kings 11:29–32.)

The Call of the Prophets

In the second half of the Old Testament, the prophets became increasingly significant as the spiritual leaders in both Israel and Judah. The golden age of prophecy in the Old Testament is generally understood to begin with the ministry of Elijah and continue through Malachi.

The prophets provide us with many good examples of how the Lord calls people into His service. Some, such as Isaiah, had a dramatic encounter with the Lord. For others, the Lord sent another prophet to communicate God's call. Others were called when they were awakened to a need among God's people. As they prayed about their concerns, the Lord opened doors for them to serve those needs.

The scriptures do not tell us how Elijah was called to the role of a prophet. They simply introduce him as going to Israel's king, Ahab, announcing that there would be no more rain in the land until he brought him word again. (See 1 Kings 17:1.) However, the call of Elijah's successor, Elisha, was different. Near the end of Elijah's life, the Lord sent him to call Elisha his successor. Elijah had fled from Jezebel and was hiding in Horeb when the Lord spoke to him about Elisha. The Lord had more work for him to do and instructed him to anoint Hazael king over Aram, Jehu king over Israel, and Elisha as his successor. (See 1 Kings 19:15–16.) Elijah only carried out the anointing of Elisha. Other prophets were sent to convey the Lord's message to the other kings.

Elisha was out working in the field when Elijah arrived. No doubt he began his day thinking about getting his work done so he could sow the field. However, by the end of the day, his world had changed. He had heard God's call through Elijah and said goodbye to his family to become Elijah's understudy. (See 1 Kings 19:19–21.)

The major writing prophets, Isaiah, Jeremiah, and Ezekiel, all write about their call. Isaiah was in the Temple when he saw a revelation of God's unveiled glory and became painfully aware of his uncleanness. When he cried out to the Lord for cleansing, the Lord took a coal of fire from the altar and cleansed his lips. With his guilt taken away and his sin atoned for, he was ready for service. When the Lord asked, "Whom shall I send? And who will go for us?" Isaiah responded, "Here am I. Send me!" (Isaiah 6:8–9 NIV).

Jeremiah tells of experiencing the Lord's call as a youth. The Lord appeared and said to him, "Before I formed you in the womb I knew you before you were born I set you apart; I appointed you as a prophet to the nations" (Jeremiah 1:5 NIV).

When Jeremiah objected that he was too young for the job, the Lord replied, "Do not say, 'I am too young. You must go to everyone I send you to and say whatever I command you. Do not be afraid of them, for I am with you and will rescue you,'" (Jeremiah 1:7–8 NIV).

Ezekiel wrote about the Lord speaking to him in Babylon and saying, "Son of man, I am sending you to the Israelites, to a rebellious nation that has rebelled against me; they and their ancestors have been in revolt against me to this very day. The people to whom I am sending you are obstinate and stubborn. Say to them, 'This is what the Sovereign LORD says'" (Ezekiel 2:3–4 NIV).

Among the minor writing prophets, Amos wrote, "I was neither a prophet nor the son of a prophet, but I was a shepherd, and I also took care of sycamore-fig trees. But the LORD took me from tending the flock and said to me, 'Go, prophesy to my people Israel'" (Amos 7:14–15 NIV). The Lord interrupted his agrarian life and called him into His service as a prophet.

Not all the prophets were called in a dramatic encounter as the prophets mentioned above. For some, their call came because they were made aware of a need among God's people and realized they could make a difference. The need began to burn itself upon their hearts to the point they felt compelled to do something about it. That was the case with Nehemiah.

He was serving in the cabinet of King Artaxerxes as his "cupbearer" when he was made aware of the conditions of his fellow Jews who were living in Jerusalem. The city's infrastructure was in total disrepair, and they lacked the leadership to change their situation. For decades, they had been attempting to repair a broken-down wall. He began to pray about this situation, and the Lord started opening doors for him to go and help. (See Nehemiah 1:2–11.) In the end, he was appointed as the governor of Jerusalem and rebuilt its walls in fifty-two days. (See Nehemiah 2–6.)

The Hebrew Words for Prophet

As mentioned above, the prophets were called from various vocations, including farmers, shepherds, priests, and the royal family. Their role was to be the Lord's spokesmen and spokeswomen, delivering His message to the people. Both the manner of their calling as well as their work as prophets serve as a good model for today's preacher. Through an encounter with the Lord, they were called to dedicate their lives to the Lord's service, and their lives were dramatically altered. They came away from those encounters with God knowing that He had called them into His service.

John Stott says a revival has never happened that was not first preceded by a revival of the preaching of the Word (Stott, The Radical Disciple 2010). That was the case with the Old Testament prophets. Throughout the Old Testament, when the people drifted away from the Lord and got into trouble, they began to cry to the Lord for help, and He sent prophets with His message.

Three Hebrew words are used for prophets in the Old Testament. They are *hozeh, rohe,* and *nabi.* While the first two words appear a limited number of times, the third word, nabi, occurs more than three hundred times. The common interpretation of this word relates it to the Akkadian verb *nabu,* which simply means "to call" (Bill T. Arnold, Bryan E. Beyer 1998). The prophets were "the called ones."

They did not preach their opinions or deliver the messages the people wanted to hear. They spoke with authority from God. Their messages came from God, and they were expected to faithfully deliver those messages to kings, the people, and surrounding nations. Because kings believed that God knew the future, they often asked the prophets to tell them about the future.

Often, their messages were global. Elijah was sent to Syrian Zarephath to be sustained by a widow during a famine. Later, he was called to anoint Hazael as the successor to Ben-Hadad as king of Aram. (See 1 Kings 19:15.) Elisha healed Naaman, the commander of Aram's armies. (See 2 Kings 5:1–19.) Jeremiah was called a "prophet to the nations" (Jeremiah 1:5 NIV). Jonah was sent to Nineveh. Daniel's ministry was in Babylon and Persia as he served as a special adviser to both Babylonian and Persian kings. He understood that God was the governor of the universe and placed kings on thrones or removed them according to His purposes. Daniel wrote, "He [God] deposes kings and raises up others" (Daniel 2:21 NIV). Later, he emphasized this truth again: "The Most High is sovereign over the kingdoms of men and gives them to anyone he wishes" (Daniel 4:17 NIV). The prophets received their commission to preach God's Word from God Himself and were sent to communicate those messages in Judah, Israel, and the surrounding nations.

The Call of the Priests

The priests served in both the Tabernacle and later temples. Their appointment began with Aaron being chosen as Israel's first high priest. God instructed Moses to anoint Aaron as a high priest, and upon his death, his son was to succeed him, and the succession of the high priest was to follow this family line. Succeeding generations of priests followed this family line until the destruction of the Second Temple by the Romans in AD 70. Although the priesthood survived the Babylonian captivity and was carried forward through the time of Christ, it ended with the destruction of the Second Temple by the Romans in AD 70.

During the time of Christ, there were so many priests living in the vicinity of Jerusalem that it was impossible to work all the priests into a rotation of service in Herod's Temple. Consequently, they were chosen by lot to serve in the Temple. As a result, some never got the opportunity to serve a rotation in the Temple during their lifetime. It was when Zechariah was chosen by lot to serve in the Temple that he encountered the angel announcing to him that he was going to have a son.

Although it was the exclusive right of priests to lead temple worship, they were not always the strongest spiritual forces in Israel. While most of them remained loyal to Yahweh even during times of apostasy, one could question if their motivation for their loyalty to Yahweh came in some measure from the fact that their jobs depended on it. Toward the end of the Old Testament, it was usually the prophets who were at the forefront of promoting spiritual renewal in the nation.

Having reviewed the call of the Old Testament leaders, we now examine how people were called into the Lord's service in the New Testament. How were Peter and the apostles, Paul, Timothy, and Luke called into the Lord's service?

The New Testament

Peter's call can be traced through at least five experiences of increasing significance, with each one being a defining moment in Peter's life. He was working in the fishing business when Jesus first invited him to become one of His disciples. It happened on the shores of the Sea of Galilee. On that occasion, Jesus invited him to become a disciple and promised him that, if he were to follow Him, He would make him a fisher for people. "'Come, follow me,' Jesus said, 'and I will send you out to fish for people'" (Matthew 4:19 NIV). In other words, Jesus's call was going to redirect his career from catching fish to saving people. Peter needed first to learn how to be a true disciple before he was ready for the next level of service.

The next major experience in his call came during the early part of Jesus's ministry when the crowds were gathering around Him. On one of those occasions, Jesus challenged His disciples to look at the needs of the folk around them. He compared the people to fields that were ready for the harvest and challenged His disciples to pray about the need for workers. Jesus said to Peter and the other disciples, "The harvest is plentiful but the workers are few. Ask the Lord of the harvest, therefore, to send out workers into his harvest field" (Matthew 9:37–38 NIV).

No doubt, in their minds the disciples began to think about what they could do to minister to these people. Some of the disciples were more adept in one area of ministry than others. Jesus's call engaged them in thinking about what they could do to serve the brokenness of these people.

The third experience in Peter's call was when Jesus chose twelve of His disciples to become apostles. Peter was chosen as one of the twelve. Following their appointment as apostles, they were sent on their first mission with the instructions to "Preach the gospel, heal the sick, raise the dead, cleanse those with leprosy, and drive out demons" (Matthew 10:7–8 NIV).

Peter's fourth significant experience occurred when Jesus was getting ready for His final journey to Jerusalem and asked the disciples who He was. The disciples mentioned that some were saying one thing about him, and others something else. Jesus asked His disciples, "What about you?" In an ah-ha moment, Peter responded, "You are the Messiah." On that occasion, Jesus changed Peter's name from Simon to Peter and prophetically told His disciples that God would build His church on him (Matthew 16:13–20 NIV).

Finally, the fifth step of Peter's call occurred after Jesus's resurrection when He spoke to Peter, three times asking him if he loved Him. Peter, filled with disappointment because of his failure and wanting to make amends for his sin, replied to Jesus that indeed he did love Jesus and would do anything for Him. Jesus simply told him to feed His sheep. In other words, Peter's job was to take care of the flock of God. (See John 21:15–19.)

In Peter's case, each phase of his calling took him to a deeper level of commitment. On the last occasion, Jesus informed him that his calling was going to cost him his life and invited Peter to suffer with Him. Ministry involves an invitation to share in the sufferings of Christ.

Paul

Sometime later, there was an up-and-coming young Pharisee from the tribe of Benjamin who was zealously persecuting Christ-followers. However, on his way to Damascus, he had a dramatic encounter with the Lord, where he met Jesus face-to-face. His life was forever changed. He began the day intent on opposing this new Christian movement and ended the day as a believer in Christ. Out of that experience came the conviction that he was set apart to take the Gospel to the Gentiles. When on trial for his faith before the mob in Jerusalem, he pointed back to his encounter with the Lord that day on the road to Damascus as the motivation for his ministry. (See Acts 22:6.) Later, when he was on trial before King Agrippa and Governor Festus at Caesarea, he again referred to that occasion as being the defining moment of his life. (See Acts 26:12.) It was this experience that gave him his purpose for life. More is discussed about Paul's call in the next chapter.

Timothy

Timothy's call to the ministry seems to have come out of Paul's method for appointing elders in the churches. On their first missionary journey, Paul and Barnabas appointed elders in the churches they had just founded. On his second missionary journey with Silas, when he came to Lystra, where he and Barnabas had founded a church a few years before, he chose Timothy as his apprentice. Likely, Paul looked for qualifications in Timothy like those included in the lists of qualifications that he later sent to Timothy and Titus to follow when they appointed elders in the churches. That list included qualifications for both elders and deacons. (See 1 Timothy 3:1–10 and Titus 1:6–9.) The elders in Lystra laid their hands on Timothy and commissioned him to go with Paul as his understudy. Timothy's call is discussed more in depth in the next chapter.

Luke

Another prominent New Testament leader is Luke, who wrote the third Gospel and the book of Acts and was more of a behind-the-scenes type of person. In Acts, Luke records the history of the expansion of the early church but does not tell us how he came to faith in Christ. All we have about Luke's conversion and a call is what we can surmise from his writings. Paul simply mentions his name in three of his letters and one time refers to him as Luke the doctor. (See Colossians 4:14.)

He appears to have first joined Paul, Silas, and Timothy at Troas on Paul's second missionary journey and traveled with them to Philippi. We can gather this by the *we* sections in Acts where Luke tells the story in the first-person plural. (See Acts 16:10.) (Some believe that Luke may have been present earlier in Acts 11:28, but not all agree with the Western text in this verse.) Luke appears to have remained at Philippi or returned home while Paul traveled on to his next stop in Thessalonica.

Luke was a physician and possibly a Gentile. In the introduction to his Gospel, he notes that he researched and recorded the life of Christ for his friend Theophilus. In Acts, he wrote about the early days of the church, the conversion of Paul, and the church's expansion into Asia Minor and Europe primarily through the ministries of Paul.

Luke does not record having any kind of any special encounter with the Lord where He was instructed to write his Gospel or the history of the early church. Rather, it seems that Luke wanted his wealthy friend, Theophilus, to know about the story of Jesus and the expansion of the church from Palestine to Asia Minor and Europe. Perhaps Luke, like Nehemiah, saw a need for a record and sought to meet that need by writing his Gospel and Acts. Without a doubt, he was inspired by the Spirit to record the stories of Jesus and the church.

Conclusion

In all these stories, we must understand that it was God who initiated the call. Sometimes His call seemed more like a command than an invitation, and the experience was dramatic. At other times, it seemed to come out of the ebb and flow of life. No doubt, there were some whom Jesus called into his service who rejected His invitation and are never heard from again. That was the case of the rich young ruler who rejected Jesus's invitation to sell his possessions and follow Him. Who knows? Perhaps he would have been appointed as one of the apostles if he had chosen to follow Jesus. Only God knows the importance of those moments in our lives.

As humans, we do not have the prerogative to initiate the special call to ministry. It must come from the Caller and His sovereign will. However, the church has the responsibility to recognize and affirm those who have the special call of God as it approves candidates for ordination. Having briefly looked at the experiences of people whom God called into His work, we now look at the manner God uses when He calls them into His work.

Questions

1. Define the special call of God.
2. Who is the source of the special call to ministry?
3. In what ways is the special call of God like a special revelation?
4. What qualified the patriarchs to receive the Lord's call?
5. Would the priesthood have demonstrated greater fidelity to the Lord if they had been selected by a special call from God like the prophets?
6. How was Paul called into ministry?
7. How was Timothy called into the ministry?
8. How is the decision to enter ministry different from the decision to enter other professions?

Bill T. Arnold, Bryan E. Beyer. (1998). *Encountering the Old Testament.* Grand Rapids, MI: Baker Book House.

Stott, J. (2010). *The Radical Disciple.* Nottingham, England: InterVarsity Press.

How God Speaks

> Those who survived the exile and are back in the province
> are in great trouble and disgrace. The wall of Jerusalem is
> broken down, and its gates have been burned with fire …
> I sat down and wept. For some days I mourned and fasted
> and prayed before the God of heaven.
>
> —Nehemiah 1:3–4 (NIV)

There are several methods that God uses to communicate His call to people. They include a dramatic moment of encounter with God, sending another person to communicate God's message, and awakening within a person the realization of a need in the Lord's work. Each method is distinctive but not necessarily exclusive with easily defined boundaries.

The boundaries frequently overlap, and the methods often complement each other, at times making it a challenge to distinguish between the three methods. At other times, they are easily distinguishable. To some extent, all of these are involved in the special call to ministry.

When I began researching the call of God, I assumed that there was primarily one way the Lord calls a person into the ministry. That is by speaking directly to them, as He spoke to Moses. However, as I listened to stories of people who have been called to the ministry and read the scriptures, I discovered the Lord uses a variety of methods to call people into His service.

There are many successful pastors and Christian leaders who did not have a dramatic moment of encounter with the Lord when they first experienced a call to the ministry. The Lord initially spoke to them indirectly, yet they understood, with conviction, that God was calling them into His work. These experiences shaped their careers. Sometimes the call came as a disruption of their lives—the failure of a marriage, the loss of a job, a major illness, or some other major event that threatened their future. In times of crisis, they turned to God, and He began to speak to them about the ministry.

As I have listened to candidates for ordination share the stories of their call, I have been impressed by how many of them sensed a calling to ministry early in life. Some chose a different path in life, but the further down their career path they traveled, the more they realized they were on the wrong path. When they began to earnestly seek the Lord's help, once again they were brought back to the idea of ministry.

It is not uncommon to hear middle-aged people pursuing ordination testify about a period when they resisted the Lord's call. As long as they resisted the Lord's call, they could not find peace. However, when they came to the place of yielding their careers to Christ's lordship, they discovered a newfound peace, and the idea of ministry began to grow in their hearts.

The Lord knows the raw material that He must work with when He calls us. He knows our history, our strengths and weaknesses, and our potential for His work. It is not uncommon for people to have reservations, fears, and misgivings about the Lord's call. They fear they will fail and are aware of personal weaknesses and question if they can ever succeed in ministry.

That was the case with Moses. He felt as though he could not speak well enough to confront Pharaoh. Yet God wanted to communicate to Pharaoh through Moses what He was about to do. Jeremiah believed he was too young and lacked the proper temperament to be "a prophet to the nations." Yet there is no other Old Testament prophet who foreshadowed the sufferings of Christ more than Jeremiah. He remained faithful under severe persecution and rejection. Paul had moments when he believed his history of persecuting the church disqualified him from a leadership role in the church, but what he discovered was that Christ was able to transform his weaknesses into some of his greatest strengths. The suffering, persecutions, and death threats that he faced by those who opposed his message did not hold him back from preaching the Gospel in hostile environments.

A Spiritual Calling

Our relationship with the Lord is foundational to hearing and understanding the Lord's call. Cultivating a vibrant relationship with the Lord is essential to understanding the will of God concerning a vocational call to ministry. When our relationship with Christ flourishes, it becomes easier for us to know and understand God's will for our careers and calling. When our relationship is weak, vacillating, and hindered through disobedience and doubts, confusion sometimes arises.

I challenge students to write out a prayer about seeking the Lord's guidance for their futures and record it in a prayer journal. Writing out our prayers enables us to reflect more deeply about what we are asking God to do for us and allows the Spirit to guide us with our petitions. Writing down our prayers allows us to go back in our journal and see how the Lord has chosen to answer our prayers in the past.

Considerations about the Call to Ministry

There are two primary considerations to keep in mind when seeking the Lord's guidance about ministry. First, the Lord expects us to utilize our gifts, talents, and experiences in life to build His kingdom and bless our world. As God's image bearers, we are designed to be channels so God's love and grace can flow from our lives. God's very nature is loving and giving, "For God so loved the world that he gave ..." (John 3:16 KJV). As His image bearers, we are designed to be conduits of His grace, allowing it to flow through us to those around us. We are not designed to be reservoirs and hoard His blessings.

When we give, we discover that it caused God's grace to flow into our lives in an even greater measure. On his final trip to Jerusalem, as Paul was leaving the Ephesian believers, he reminded them that for three years he had provided the income for himself and his team while he ministered to them. In pointing this out, he quoted Jesus as saying, "It is more blessed to give than to receive" (Acts 20:35 NIV). At its core, ministry involves giving and blessings others.

A second consideration involved in the call to ministry is the question, "Has the Lord providentially placed me in a particular place or circumstance, at a specific time for His purpose?" If we are alert to what is going on around us, we sometimes discover the Lord places us in a particular situation at a particular time to reveal His purpose and call us into His work. In the Old Testament, Esther's uncle Mordecai pointed out that perhaps she was in the royal house, "for such a time as this" (Esther 4:14 NIV). There are times when we are strategically placed in a particular situation so the Lord can accomplish His purpose in us. Let us examine the three methods God uses to call people into the ministry.

The Dramatic Encounter

The first way God calls us is the dramatic moment encounter. The Bible is filled with stories of people who experienced God's call in this manner. From the moment of their encounter, they recognized they were called into the Lord's service. God dramatically intersected their lives, and their plans for the future were radically altered.

This happened to Moses. Moses was born during a time of fierce persecution of the Hebrew people, causing them to cry out to God for help. When the Hebrew people were told by the Pharaoh to throw all their baby boys into the river, they cried out to the Lord for help, and He took notice of their situation by sending Moses.

Moses's mother, Jochebed, was a resourceful woman who came up with an innovative way to save her newborn son. Instead of throwing him into the water as commanded by the authorities, she made a basket of papyrus, covered it with a waterproof coating, placed him in it, and hid it among the bulrushes along the water's edge. She then sent her daughter Miriam to watch her baby brother.

Through God's providence, Pharaoh's daughter just happened to come to that location to bathe. As she was walking along the river's edge, she caught sight of a baby boy in a basket and had the infant brought to her. Her heart went out to this baby, and she fell in love with him.

In a moment of quick thinking, Miriam, Moses's sister, ran up and offered to help her find a woman to nurse the baby for her. The Egyptian princess took Miriam up on her offer, and Moses's mother was brought to the princess. The Egyptian princess paid Jochebed to nurse Moses until he was old enough to live with her in the palace. On one side of the coin, all of this appeared to be a coincidence—a case of being in the right place at the right time. That is the way it looked to the princess. On the other side, this was the providential hand of the Lord answering the prayers of the Hebrew people about their plight.

There are many times in our lives when the Lord's providence goes unrecognized at the moment. It is only in retrospect that we recognize the Lord was with us all along, and His marvelous hand was at work.

Moses never forgot the love and protection of his mother and sister. As he grew older, he came to realize that his life had been spared for a purpose. One day, after he was grown, he saw a Hebrew being beaten by an Egyptian slave master and intervened. In the process, he killed the Egyptian, buried him in the sand, and hoped that no one would notice. When he realized that his action of killing the Egyptian was known, he knew that he was in trouble.

He fled east, eventually stopping in Sinai at the house of Jethro the priest. There, he settled into a shepherd's life, married one of Jethro's daughters, and began raising his two sons. He was about forty years old when he fled Egypt and, for the next forty years, lived a shepherd's life. No doubt he was planning to live out the rest of his days in Sinai. However, his life was changed in a dramatic moment.

He began his day as he normally did, by watching the sheep while they grazed. However, during the day, he noticed something unusual—a bush was on fire but not being consumed by the fire. His curiosity led him to investigate what was happening, and when he did, he heard a voice calling to him. He was told not to come near the bush and to take off his sandals because he was on holy ground.

The Lord said to Moses that He was the God of his ancestors Abraham, Isaac, and Jacob and that He had heard the prayers of the Israelites and saw their suffering. Now He was sending Moses to deliver the Hebrew people. When Moses inquired about His name, the Lord answered Moses that His name was *Yahweh*, or I AM. (See Exodus 3:11–15.) He continued, "So now, go. I am sending you to Pharaoh to bring my people the Israelites out of Egypt" (Exodus 3:10 NIV).

Moses's initial reaction was concern about his inadequacies. He did not feel that he could speak well enough to go before Pharaoh. He was also afraid the people would not believe him and that Pharaoh would not take him seriously. Because of his doubts, Moses asked the Lord to send Aaron with him. The Lord accommodated Moses's request by sending his brother Aaron as his spokesman.

The Lord confirmed His call to Moses with a couple of miracles. First, when Moses threw his staff on the ground, it became a snake. When he picked it up, it was changed back into a staff. Next, when he put his hand inside his clothing, it became leprous. The second time he put his hand into his clothing, it was completely healed. (See Exodus 4:2–7.) Moses's life was radically altered that day. The Lord had invaded his world, and his life would never be the same.

Mark grew up in a pastor's home and realized early on that he was called to the ministry. In college, he was part of a vocal group that traveled around the country singing in churches. Following college, he enrolled in seminary but was not serious about ministry or preaching. During his first year in seminary, he put forth just enough effort to get decent grades but did not seek to give his best in his studies.

Then one day, all of that changed. He came to his preaching class, found a seat in the rear of the classroom, and settled in to listen to one of his classmates give a sermon. He planned to do his evaluation of the sermon and continue his day as usual.

When his classmate stood to deliver his sermon, suddenly he buried his face in his hands and began to sob uncontrollably. Now everyone's attention was focused on the speaker. Eventually, he was able to gain enough composure to explain to the class what was happening. Every time he had to stand before an audience to speak, he was terrified and paralyzed with stage fright. Yet he felt the Lord had called him to preach, and he did not know what to do about it.

Mark was processing all of this when suddenly the Spirit whispered to him, reminding him that he had no problem with stage fright. It was easy for him to stand before an audience and speak. He had traveled the country and been in front of hundreds of audiences. Yet he was not taking this class seriously by not giving his best efforts in this preaching class.

Mark said, "I knew the Lord had spoken to me, and I left class that day a different man. The Spirit had gotten my attention, and I resolved from that day forward, with the Lord's help, I would become the best preacher I could be."

Paul

A millennium and a half after Moses, in a different context and under radically different circumstances, another man had a dramatic encounter with the Lord. He was an up-and-coming young Jew who had studied under one of the best religious teachers of his day. He could trace his heritage back to the tribe of Benjamin and was a member of one of the strictest religious groups of his day. He was also convinced that the teachings of another Jewish teacher were heretical. This young Jew named Saul was from the city of Tarsus and committed to purging out the scourge of a false teacher named Jesus. In Jerusalem, he was present holding the coats of those who stoned Stephen, one of Jesus's followers. (See Acts 7:58.)

He had just gotten papers from the authorities in Jerusalem authorizing him to arrest any Christians he found in the synagogues in Damascus and bring them, bound, to Jerusalem for trial. However, on the way, something happened. He was struck off his horse by a bolt of lightning and left blind. At that moment, he heard a voice speaking to him, "Saul, Saul why do you persecute me?" (Acts 9:4 NIV).

He asked who it was that was speaking to him, only to learn it was Jesus whom he was persecuting. For the next three days, he was blind and thought about what had just happened. A few days later, one of Jesus's followers named Ananias came to anoint him for healing for his blindness and baptize him into the Christian faith. (See Acts 9:13–19.) Saul came away from that encounter realizing that he was set apart for a ministry to the Gentiles. His life was never the same.

Is this kind of experience typical for those who are called into the ministry? Some share stories of a dramatic experience in which the Lord called them into the ministry. Jim (not his real name) was finishing his third year of engineering school, anticipating a career in engineering. However, in a Sunday-evening service, he was moved to go forward for a time of prayer after the sermon. While in prayer, the Lord seemed to speak directly to him, as if a person were speaking audibly to him. He asked Jim if he would be willing to forego his ambitions for a career in engineering and follow God's plans for his life. Because of his growing relationship with Christ, it was easy for him to say yes to the Lord.

He was shocked by what came next. The Lord asked him if he would preach. Before that evening, he had never given serious thought to being a preacher.

A few weeks after that experience, his pastor gave him his first opportunity to preach. That was when reality set in. If he were to be successful at preaching, he had a lot of work to do. Speaking did not come easily for him. It took him a lot of work and time to prepare a sermon, and then preaching did not seem to be in his wheelhouse of strengths. Over the next few months, he withdrew from engineering school and enrolled in Bible college.

That encounter with the Lord kept him focused on this calling throughout life. Several outstanding opportunities would later come his way that would have taken him out of the ministry, and he turned them down because of his encounter with the Lord in that Sunday-night service. There were upheavals in his life caused by extremely tough church decisions. In those moments of testing and trial, his experience on that Sunday evening kept him focused on ministry and answering God's call.

A person must be grounded in the conviction of their calling if they are to survive the upheavals that sometimes come in ministry. Hard times will come, and during those times of testing, there is the temptation is to leave the ministry. The conviction of the call is what keeps a person in the ministry during these testing times. There are examples in scripture where people turned away from the ministry during hard times.

When Paul wrote his second letter to Timothy, Demas had left the ministry. (See 2 Timothy 4:10.) Earlier in his letters to Colossae and Philemon, Demas, along with Luke and Mark, were serving alongside Paul in ministry. However, by the time of his last letter to Timothy, Demas had left the ministry.

Sending Another Person

A second way the Lord uses to call a person into His work is by sending one of his servants to communicate God's call. He sent the prophet Samuel to anoint Saul as Israel's first king. (See 1 Samuel 9:15–17.) He later sent Samuel to anoint David as Israel's second king. (See 1 Samuel 16:1–13.) Both were surprised when the prophet showed up and informed them they had been chosen to be Israel's king. There is no indication that before Samuel's anointing, Saul had a prior awareness that he would become Israel's first king. It was a similar experience with David. He was out in the field taking care of sheep when Samuel came to his house to anoint him as Israel's next king.

After Elijah's spectacular victory on Mount Carmel, when he ordered that all the prophets of Baal be put to death, Jezebel, the king's wife, was enraged by Elijah's actions and called for his life. He fled to the desert, thinking his life and ministry were over and that he should go into hiding. However, the Lord had more work for him to do. He told Elijah to anoint Hazael as king of Aram, Jehu as the next king of Israel, and Elisha as his successor. (See 1 Kings 19:15–16.)

When Elijah left the desert and arrived at his house, Elisha was in the field plowing. There is no indication that Elisha had any premonition that Elijah would show up. Elijah approached Elisha and threw his outer garment upon him. This move symbolized that Elijah's prophetic office was being transferred to Elisha. At that moment, the Spirit descended upon Elisha and changed him. His response was to kill the oxen he was using to plow and use the plowing instruments as firewood for a sacrifice. That day, Elisha became Elijah's apprentice and followed him until the day Elijah was taken into heaven in a whirlwind. Before Elijah was taken to heaven, Elisha requested that he receive a double portion of Elijah's spirit.

There are a couple of key lessons to be learned from this story. First, Elisha's call was first communicated to Elijah by God. Although Elisha lived near a school of prophets, there is no indication that before that occasion Elisha was associated with the group. Second, when Elisha realized that God had called him, he spared nothing in answering His call. For him, there was no turning back. He sacrificed the oxen he was using to plow and used the plowing instruments as firewood for the sacrifice. In contrast to Elisha's actions were the actions of a rich young ruler who came to Jesus asking about the way to eternal life. When Jesus told him to sell all his possessions, give the proceeds to the poor, and follow Him, the cost was too high for this young man, and he turned away from Jesus. (See Matthew 19:21.)

One day, I was at lunch with a group of pastors and asked one of them to tell us about his call to preach. His response surprised everyone at the table when he nodded in the direction of the district superintendent and said, "He called me to preach." Most assumed, as I did at that time, that it is God who speaks directly to a person when He calls them into the ministry.

He continued saying that at the time, the district superintendent was his pastor, and they lived in another state. He was a high school teacher and cotaught a Sunday school class with his pastor. One Sunday, he showed up for church expecting to teach his Sunday school class when his pastor met him at the door and asked, "Will you be willing to drive across town to fill in for my son who is scheduled to preach? He is sick and can't go this morning."

He was caught off guard by his pastor's question and responded, "I'm not a preacher. I have never preached before in my life. Besides, I don't have a sermon."

His pastor was persistent. "Why don't you just go and give them your testimony?"

He said, "I paused for a few moments and thought, *I can do that. I can give my testimony*. So, I agreed."

He drove across town that Sunday morning, and when it came time for the sermon, he was introduced as the guest preacher and gave them his testimony. After the service, he was caught by surprise when the church treasurer handed him a check for preaching and asked, "You will be back to preach for us again tonight, won't you?"

He concluded, "I've been preaching ever since that Sunday morning."

After Paul's dramatic conversion experience, he returned to his home in Tarsus and lived there for some time. Later, when Barnabas was sent by the Jerusalem Church to check on the Christians in Antioch, he traveled on to Tarsus to search for Paul. When he found him, he brought Paul back and introduced him to the church at Antioch, where they ministered together for a year. (See Acts 11:25–26.) Later, he and Paul took a gift from the Antioch Christians to Jerusalem and returned to Antioch. It was while they were in Antioch that the Spirit moved upon the hearts of the believers to separate Barnabas and Paul and commission them as missionaries to Cyprus and Asia Minor. What would church history look like if Barnabas had not sought out Paul and reintroduced him to the church? I am sure it would be different.

Timothy

Another example of God working through one of His servants to communicate a call to ministry is the story of Paul and Timothy. On their first missionary journey, Paul and Barnabas evangelized in Timothy's hometown along with the neighboring towns. It was there that Paul was stoned and dragged out of the city for dead. However, after he regained his strength, he went to the next city and continued evangelizing. On his second missionary journey with Silas, he revisited some of those churches.

When they arrived at Lystra, Paul discovered a young man named Timothy with a good reputation among the churches in that area. (See Acts 16:1–3.) With the affirmation of the church leaders, Paul chose Timothy as an understudy and took him along as his apprentice. There is no indication that Timothy had a dramatic moment experience like Paul.

Christian leaders should be alert to the Spirit's promptings and be ready to challenge young people with good potential for leadership to consider entering the ministry. Not everyone is called to be a minister, but more people would be in ministry if they received encouragement at the right times.

A word of caution is appropriate here. It is important to stay in step with the Spirit's leading. There are times when an older person simply wishes for a young person to go into ministry, and that desire may not be in harmony with the Spirit's promptings. This can bring unnecessary confusion to a young person and at times cause them to misunderstand the Lord's call for their lives. However, under the leadership of the Spirit, church leaders should be alert to young people who have leadership potential and challenge them to pray about considering ministry as a career.

Awakening to a Need

A third way the Lord communicates His call to ministry is by awakening a person to a particular need in the Lord's work. They happen to be in a certain place, at a particular time, under special circumstances, and their attention is drawn to serving a particular need. If given the opportunity, they feel they can make a difference. The awareness of that need begins to embed itself into their thoughts and minds to the point they feel compelled to do something about it.

Nehemiah was serving in the king's cabinet as his cupbearer. The cupbearer was a key person in the king's cabinet and first sampled the king's food and wine to make sure it was not poisoned. He was the equivalent of a leading secret service agent for the king, requiring the king's trust.

In that position, he had the opportunity to learn firsthand about the inner workings of the government and finance. Not only did Nehemiah have a good understanding of administration, but he also had a good aptitude for it. Things were going well for this exile until, one day, he learned about the condition of the people back in his homeland. His brother had just visited Jerusalem and told him about the horrible living conditions in Jerusalem. The city walls were broken down, and the people were vulnerable to attacks from raiding bands of hoodlums. The infrastructure was crumbling, making it a horrible place to live.

That was not the city he had heard about from his ancestors. The condition of Jerusalem distressed Nehemiah to the point that he could not get it out of his mind. If given an opportunity, he could make a difference, and he began praying about it.

This is Nehemiah's prayer when he learned about the horrible conditions in Jerusalem:

> LORD, the God of heaven, the great and awesome God, who keeps his covenant of love with those who love him and keep his commandments, let your ear be attentive and your eyes open to hear the prayer your servant is praying before you day and night for your servants, the people of Israel. I confess the sins we Israelites, including myself and my father's family, have committed against you. We have acted very wickedly toward you. We have not obeyed the commands, decrees, and laws you gave your servant Moses.
>
> Remember the instruction you gave your servant Moses, saying, "If you are unfaithful, I will scatter you among the nations, but if you return to me and obey my commands, then even if your exiled people are at the farthest horizon, I will gather them from there and bring them to the place I have chosen as a dwelling for my Name."
>
> They are your servants and your people, whom you redeemed by your great strength and your mighty hand. Lord, let your ear be attentive to the prayer of this your servant and to the prayer of your servants who delight in revering your name. Give your servant success today by granting him favor in the presence of this man. (Nehemiah 1:5–11 NIV)

Soon, the king noticed a change in Nehemiah's countenance and inquired what was bothering him. Nehemiah candidly replied that it was the conditions in his homeland in Jerusalem. The city was in a state of disrepair and needed drastic changes. When the king asked Nehemiah what he could do for him, Nehemiah responded by requesting permission to go to Jerusalem and oversee the rebuilding of its infrastructure. As a result, the king authorized him to head up the work and provided him with the resources.

When Nehemiah arrived in Jerusalem, he discovered that for decades they had struggled to rebuild the walls. The people's morale was low, and their work was hampered by attacks from their enemies, making the task of finishing repairs on the walls daunting. Although Ezra had been in the city for some time, leading spiritual reform, the living conditions were deplorable. However, in fifty-two days after his arrival, Nehemiah finished rebuilding the walls. God provided a man for His work!

After the walls were restored, he teamed up with Ezra, built a platform, assembled the people in Jerusalem, and had Ezra read the Law to the people. (See Nehemiah 8.) The public reading of the Law to the people was a new way of doing worship—instead of worship being focused on animal sacrifices, the reading of scripture was now included. When Ezra read the Law to the people, Nehemiah had Levites placed among the people to help them understand what it meant. This is the first time in the Bible when the scriptures are read to the people in a public setting. (Nehemiah 8:3–4; Walton, Matthews, & Chavalas, 2000).

Probably, the public reading of scripture began in the synagogues during the Babylonian captivity and over time became commonplace in synagogue worship. Both Ezra and Nehemiah recognized the value of this practice and carried it back to Jerusalem.

Nehemiah continued as governor and worked with Ezra to bring about spiritual reform. His call was initiated simply by learning about a need in his ancestral city and believing he could make a difference. In the end, Nehemiah is listed among the writing prophets.

There are times when God's call follows this pattern, and we find ourselves in a situation that may not necessarily be because of our choosing. However, in those circumstances, our attention is drawn to a particular need, and we realize that we can make a difference if given the opportunity. As the doors of opportunity open for us, we seek to make a difference in the situation.

After His ascension into heaven, Jesus expected His followers to become His hands, feet, and voice to serve the needs of a broken world. Christians all around the world discover that as they serve the needs of people around them, it is not unusual for them to sense they are where they are supposed to be, doing what God has called them to do. God does not necessarily expect us to do extraordinary feats. Rather, it is often the simple acts of faithful service that God uses to accomplish something much greater than what we can imagine. That was the case with JoeAnn.

JoeAnn grew up as the adopted daughter of distant relatives who expected her to complete college. After high school, she enrolled in a state college but soon realized she was in the wrong place. Later that year, a group of young men from a small Bible college stopped by their home and invited her and her brother to attend Bible college with them.

The next fall, she decided to give Bible college a try. At Bible college, she began to grow spiritually and soon decided to complete her education there. As graduation approached, she was anxious about what to do next. When her district superintendent visited the campus, he discussed with her classmates various possibilities at several churches. Finally, at the end of his visit, he asked JoeAnn if she would consider moving to Memphis to reopen a closed church. The district would give her a small salary. Although she did not feel called to preach, she did have a heart for people, and there were no other options open for her, so she took him up on the offer.

In Memphis, she began refurbishing the church, giving it a new coat of paint. Once the church was painted, she opened the doors to hold her first Sunday school class. On the first Sunday, no one showed up. In her naiveté, she thought that all she needed to do was to open the church doors and people would come. But that did not happen. She then began inviting children to come to her Sunday school class and discovered they were reluctant to attend because they did not have suitable clothes. She then began using a portion of her small salary to buy used clothes for the children.

By the second year, her small church had grown to the size where the district superintendent was able to send a pastor. But something had happened to JoeAnn during that first year—her love for the downtrodden people in Memphis had grown to the point she felt compelled to continue ministering to the children.

Over the next several years, she continued ministering to the downtrodden folk in Memphis, and her flock grew and grew. Later, she met and married her husband, who also had a love for the people, and together they raised their four children. They also provided a home for seventy-five foster children besides hundreds of other children who lived with them for short periods.

Eventually, she organized and launched the Neighborhood Christian Centers to serve the downtrodden people in Memphis and served as its director for twenty-six years. By the time she retired, the NCC was raising nearly a million dollars annually from private donations and ministering to 125,000 people (Ballard and Currier 2005).

JoAnn did not have a dramatic encounter with the Lord like Moses or Paul. However, she allowed the Lord to enlarge her heart to see the needs of the broken people that surrounded her. She cultivated her love for people until it intertwined itself with her heart, to the point that she felt compelled to serve those needs. Her calling came as the Lord led her step by step in the pathway of ministry.

Often a Combination of the Three Manners

We have examined three distinctive ways the Lord chooses to speak to people when He calls them into ministry. Sometimes He uses a combination of two or three of these ways. Even after his dramatic encounter with the Lord, Moses asked God to send his brother Aaron to further confirm His call. (See Exodus 4:27.) This built Moses's confidence in the Lord's providential care of his mission.

After Paul's dramatic conversion on the Damascus road, it was Barnabas who went to Tarsus, sought him out, and reintroduced him to the church. It was from the church in Antioch that the Spirit separated Barnabas and Paul for their first missionary journey, sending them west with the gospel.

We do not go to heaven alone. We need the help and fellowship of our brothers and sisters in Christ. This is also true in the work of ministry.

Surrendering to the Lordship of Christ

When we obediently follow God's leadership for our lives, He continues to bless our steps of obedience with more guidance. While we cannot always see the end goals, God does, and He gives us enough direction for the next steps in this journey of faith. Each step taken in obedience to God's call builds confidence for the next step.

Submission to Christ's lordship is essential to understanding the call to ministry. In the next chapter, we examine how to find God's will and direction for our lives. The more we open our lives to Christ's lordship and courageously follow His leadership, the greater is our sense of inner well-being and peace. How do we find God's will for our lives?

Questions

1. What are the three methods God uses to call people into His work?
2. What method did God use to call Moses? Who in the New Testament had a similar experience?
3. What method did God use to call Elisha? Who in the New Testament had a similar experience?
4. Read the story of Jeremiah's call (Jeremiah 1:4–10). What were some of his reservations about what the Lord was calling him to do?
5. What method did God use to call Nehemiah? Who in the New Testament had a similar experience?
6. What is essential to a clear understanding of our call?
7. Do you think the call to the ministry is a lifetime calling? Why?

Ballard, J., & Currier, S. 2005. *I Belong Here.* Memphis, TN: The Master Design.

Smith, M. B. 1991. *Knowing God's Will.* Downers Grove, IL: InterVarsity Press.

Walton, J., Matthews, V., & Chavalas, M. 2000. *The IVP Bible Background Commentary Old Testament.* Downers Grove, IL: InteVarsity Press.

CHAPTER

8 *Seeking Divine Guidance*

"You will seek me and find me when you seek me with
all your heart."

—Jeremiah 29:13 (NIV)

Vibrant Christians routinely make good spiritual decisions in life. The
practice of making good spiritual decisions is linked to practicing the
spiritual disciplines. Numerous other factors are also associated with good
decisions, but at the center of a pattern of good decisions is a pattern of
carefully seeking the Lord's leadership of our lives and giving attention
to our spiritual well-being. If our spiritual life is anemic and weak, we
are exposed to the winds of influence from the world that blow us first
in one direction and then another. Paul wrote we are caught up in those

circumstances we are like "infants, tossed back and forth by the waves, and blown here and there by every wind of teaching and by the cunning and craftiness of people in their deceitful scheming" (Ephesians 4:14 NIV).

Earlier, he had written to the Corinthian believers that because of their anemic spiritual condition, they were able only to digest milk and not meat. (See 1 Corinthians 3:2.) His challenge was for them to grow up and become strong in their faith. Spiritual growth is associated with the practice of the spiritual disciplines. Five of these disciplines are discussed below. More could be added to the list, but in the interest of time and space, only five are discussed to illustrate that when we get serious with seeking the Lord's leadership in our lives, He begins to fill our lives with the sanctifying grace of His Spirit.

When making important decisions, where do we go for spiritual guidance? How can we make good decisions and avoid bad ones? How do we know what is the right choice? This chapter is about seeking divine guidance.

Spiritual disciplines are those habits that Christians regularly practice as they develop their relationship with Christ and become familiar with His voice and will. In practicing them, we invite the Holy Spirit to have an increasing influence in our lives. These spiritual routines make it easier to recognize God's voice and follow His leadership. However, like anything worthwhile, they require an investment of time and effort and must become habits in our lives.

In teaching His disciples about what it means to be a part of His flock, Jesus said, "I have come that they may have life, and have it to the full" (John 10:10 NIV). In this passage, Jesus compares His followers to sheep and promises that those who faithfully follow Him can expect to experience the fullness of spiritual life. Those who regularly engage in the spiritual disciplines discover that their relationship with Christ flourishes and becomes an increasing source of joy, satisfaction, and peace. In the fold of the Good Shepherd, His followers are led into fields of good pasture. They discover it is easier to discern God's will and experience greater courage to make the right choices. They become more familiar with the voice of the Lord.

The Will of God

Christians often ask, "How can I find the will of God for my life?" "Is the Lord calling me into the ministry?" "How can I know whether or not I should marry this person?" "How can I find God's will about whether I should take this job?" These and similar questions lead us to seek divine guidance from the Lord.

God is interested in every aspect of our lives. He is interested not only in our relationship with Him but also in our vocations and how we spend our time. He desires for our lives to glorify Him and for us to accomplish the purpose for which we are on this earth. As His image bearers, we are responsible for the stewardship of our time and talents.

The expression *finding God's will* is used here to refer to receiving direction from God about the decisions we make. Paul writes about God's perfect will. "Do not conform to the pattern of this world but be transformed by the renewing of your mind. Then you will be able to test and approve what God's will is—his good, pleasing and perfect will" (Romans 12:2 NIV). What does the Bible say about God's will? What does the expression *the will of God* mean?

The first way the expression *the will of God* is used in scripture is to express God's immutable will. That means there is nothing on earth that can stop God's will from being done. For example, in his sermon at Pentecost, Peter refers to Jesus having been delivered up "by the deliberate will and plan of God" (Act 2:23 NIV). This means that it was God's will for Jesus to become the sacrifice for our sins and the Savior of the world, and nothing in heaven and earth could prevent God's immutable will from being done. In this text, the Greek word used for "will" is *boule*. When *boule* is used in the New Testament, it is frequently used to refer to God's immutable will.

The second way the expression *will of God* is used in scripture is to express God's desire that requires the cooperation of humans. For example, in the Lord's Prayer, Jesus taught us to pray, "Your will be done on earth, as it is in heaven" (Matthew 6:10 NIV). In this prayer, the Greek word translated "will" is *thelema*. In contrast to *boule*, this word is used to convey God's "desire" as opposed to his "immutable will" and requires the cooperation of human beings.

Another place this word is used in this way is in Paul's first letter to the church at Thessalonica. He wrote, "It is God's will that you should be sanctified: that you should avoid sexual immorality" (1 Thessalonians 4:3 NIV). In other words, it was God's desire for the Thessalonian believers to live lives that were set apart for God's glory. Not all believers in the congregation at Thessalonica were living in that manner; hence his admonition to live holy lives as Christ followers.

In the next chapter, Paul uses a similar expression, "Give thanks in all circumstances; for this is God's will for you in Christ Jesus" (1 Thessalonians 5:18 NIV). Here Paul means that it is God's desire for Christians to be thankful regardless of their circumstances. In both instances, Paul admonishes the Thessalonian believers regarding God's desire for them.

Thus, when the expression *the will of God* is used, we must take into consideration its context. Does it mean God's immutable will? Or is it referring to God's desire for us? In the discussion below, the expression *the will of God* is used in the second sense.

There are people whom the Lord calls to preach who refuse to answer His call. That was the case with Jonah. He was called to preach to the people in Nineveh but chose to go in the opposite direction. It was not until he spent three days in the belly of a big fish that he changed his mind.

In the story of Deborah in the Old Testament, God sent her to Barak, asking him to lead the armies of Israel into battle against the army of Jabin, the Canaanite king. However, Barak lacked courage and agreed to lead the army only if Deborah would accompany him. Deborah warned him that if he set limits on God, it would be a woman and not him who would be credited with the victory.

When God calls a person into the ministry, there may be the temptation to resist His call or an unwillingness to allow Him to send us to certain places with specific tasks. If this is the situation, we will never experience the fullness of God's peace and joy until we answer His call. If we do not answer His call, in the end, our lives will be shortchanged of God's full blessings.

Responsibility

God does not treat us like we are puppets on strings. As His image bearers, we are given a measure of freedom and the opportunity to participate in the work of building His kingdom. Paul refers to himself as a "co-worker with God" (2 Corinthians 6:1 NIV). When we faithfully follow God's leadership, our choices contribute on some level to building the Lord's kingdom. On the other hand, when we make unwise choices and resist God's will by being disobedient and unfaithful servants, we hinder the Lord's work.

Jesus illustrates this principle in the parable of the wise and foolish servants. (See Matthew 25:14–30.) In that parable, a wealthy man took a long journey, and before he left, he called in three of his servants and gave each of them a certain amount of responsibility while he was away. They were expected to manage their resources wisely.

While he was away, two of his servants put his resources to good use and increased their master's wealth. When their master returned, they had doubled his resources and were praised for their work. One was given even more responsibility. However, the third servant locked up his master's wealth and waited for him to return. Upon his return, he condemned that servant and took what had been given and gave it to another servant. In this parable, Jesus taught that when we use our talents to build His kingdom, they tend to multiply. On the other hand, when we fail to use them, they are taken from us and given to others.

This brings us back to the question; how can we find God's will? We need the Lord's help as we seek to make good decisions. How can we know whether an impression is God's will? Blane Smith notes that God's voice is often louder and more dramatic in the early days of our Christian walk and becomes less dramatic as we mature as Christians. When we are young in the faith, the Lord often speaks to us more directly and plainly than He does after we have walked with Him for several years.

Smith points out that this is not because God loves us less. Rather, it is because our relationship with Him has matured, and it is easier for us to understand and follow His will. Jesus said, "My sheep hear my voice" (John 10:27 KJV). As we follow Him, we become more familiar with His voice.

I grew in a farming community. A mile to the west of our farm was my paternal grandfather's farm. A mile to north was my maternal grandfather's farm. I could see both of their farms from our barn. Both of my grandfathers had small dairy operations. In the early mornings and late afternoons during the summers, when the wind was blowing in the right direction, I could hear them call their cows to the milking barn. One day when I was visiting with my grandfather at milking time, I asked him if I could call his cows, and he gave me permission. However, when I called the cows, they ignored my voice and continued grazing. However, a few minutes later, my grandfather called them, and they stopped grazing and began walking toward the barn. What was the difference? The cows recognized his voice and not mine. That is the way it is with our relationship with the Lord. The longer we walk in obedience with Christ, the easier it becomes to recognize His voice.

As our relationship with the Lord matures, we learn to trust that inner voice and the peace that it brings when our decisions are in harmony with God's will. When we do not experience that peace, it causes us to pause and search further for God's will. A couple of examples from the New Testament illustrates this principle.

New Testament Examples

When Paul chose Timothy as his apprentice in ministry, he effectively thrust Timothy into the ministry. How did Paul make this choice?

At the time, the church was rapidly expanding to the west. Paul needed an apprentice to work with him. The scriptures do not indicate that Paul heard a dramatic voice telling him to choose Timothy. Instead, when he and Silas arrived at Lystra, they met young Timothy, who had a good reputation among the churches in the region. His mother, Eunice, was a devout Jew and believer, as was his grandmother Lois. (See Acts 16.) Paul recognized that Timothy had the qualities and character that indicated good potential for the ministry. The elders at Lystra agreed with Paul's assessment and gave their approval to his choice of Timothy. (See Acts 16:1–3 and 2 Timothy 1:6.)

Because Timothy's father was a Gentile, he had not been circumcised. In order not to offend the Jewish congregations in the synagogues where Paul typically first went, Timothy was circumcised so as not to hinder the gospel message in the synagogues. The irony of this is that Paul and Silas were on a mission to deliver letters from the Jerusalem Council that stated, among other things, circumcision was not necessary for Christian believers.

Throughout the remainder of the New Testament, Timothy was a faithful Christian leader. Paul's choice was a good one. He certainly must have had the leadership of the Spirit in this crucial decision.

A second example is Luke, the author of the third Gospel and the book of Acts. He first appears in the Bible with Paul, Silas, and Timothy at Troas a short time after Timothy joined them. Initially, Paul intended to take Silas and Timothy and go northeast into Bithynia, but he was constrained by the Spirit. As a result, he went down to Troas on the Aegean Sea to wait for direction from the Spirit.

While waiting for direction at Troas, two important things happened. First, Luke appeared for the first time in the New Testament. Second, Paul had a vision of a man from Macedonia asking him to bring the gospel to Europe. As a result, the gospel was preached in Europe for the first time. (See Acts 16:9–10.) Paul took Silas, Timothy, and Luke and crossed the Aegean Sea into Europe.

In retrospect, the decision to go down to Troas and wait on direction from the Spirit was strategic because it was at Troas that Luke joined Paul. Luke was present with Paul, Silas, and Timothy is inferred by the *we* sections in Acts in which Luke wrote about their experiences in the first-person plural. This decision has blessed the church for two thousand years because Luke compiled the third Gospel and the book of Acts. Without his Gospel, we would be missing much of the narrative about Jesus's birth, along with several other important events in Jesus's life. Without Acts, we would not have a history of the early church.

What prompted Luke to compile his Gospel for his friend Theophilus? Did he hear a voice from heaven telling him to write about the story of Jesus and send it to his friend? What motivated him to follow with a history of the young church, the Acts of the apostles? The apostle John received a direct word from Jesus to write down what he saw while exiled on Patmos. (See Revelation 1:12–13.)

Perhaps Luke's wealthy friend, Theophilus, may have recently become a Christian convert and needed to learn more about the story of Christ and the growth of the church. At any rate, Luke followed his Gospel with the story of the young church as it expanded westward into Asia Minor and Europe.

When Luke wrote his two books, he could not have imagined the impact they would have on the young church—that his work would be read, reread, and studied by millions and millions of believers over two thousand years. But God knew! Perhaps at the forefront of Luke's thinking at the time was a desire to help his friend understand who Jesus was and how the church had spread from Jerusalem into the Roman world. It may have just seemed like the prudent thing to do to help his friend grow as a disciple. However, God had a much grander purpose in mind. In the end, the church has been immeasurably blessed with Luke's compilation of his Gospel and Acts. God said to Isaiah, "My ways are higher than your ways and my thoughts than your thoughts" (Isaiah 55:9 NIV). God's purposes are often beyond human comprehension. The metanarrative of what God is accomplishing in our lives is often beyond our grasp. Only God knows the significance of our faithful service.

In hindsight, it is often easy to see the providential leadership of the Lord's hand of guidance. When decisions are made in faith, it is impossible to see the consequences of those decisions—but God does. That is why it is important to regularly seek His guidance and follow the voice of His Spirit.

Christ's Lordship over Our Lives

People are sometimes confused about whether they are called to the ministry. At times, the underlying cause is an unwillingness to submit to Christ's lordship over their lives. In interviewing candidates for ministry, it is not unusual to hear them talk about initially resisting the Lord's call. Their ambitions stood in the way of God's call and overrode His voice. However, while they resisted His call, they could never find peace.

When limits are set on what we allow God's call to include, it brings confusion and robs us of peace. Sometimes it takes a major upheaval in our lives to turn us toward God, as Jonah experienced. However, as we refuse to listen to His voice over time, the call becomes weaker. What is there within us that causes us to resist God?

Origin of Resistance

Resistance to God's lordship over us is as old as humanity. It can be traced back to the Fall in the Garden of Eden. As humans, we were created to find ultimate joy and fulfillment through our relationship with our Creator. We were designed for God to be at the center of our lives. The greatest moments of joy, peace, and happiness for Adam living in the garden came at the end of the day when the Lord God came down to walk with him in the "cool of the day" (Genesis 3:8 KJV).

Satan's strategy in tempting Eve was to drive a wedge between her and her Creator and cut off the source of her joy. His lie was that she could find a new level of freedom by rebelling against her Creator. He suggested that "you will be like God" (Genesis 3:5 NIV). In other words, she would become her own god and be free to choose whatever destiny she desired.

However, her rebellion brought catastrophic results. When she removed herself from the lordship of her Creator, she made herself a slave to self and sin. After their sin, the first pair discovered that instead of gaining more freedom and joy, they were robbed of both their freedom and joy. They lost their paradise and peace and became the slaves of sin. The immediate result was their spiritual death and ultimately their physical death. That is always the end of sin. The only way to escape this spiritual death was for someone to rescue them.

It is God's grace that redeems us from sin and death. The rebellion experienced in our souls is so crippling that without God's grace, we are unable to find our way back to God. The sin in which we are born is traced back to the sin of our first parents. When Adam and Eve sinned, they passed along to every member of humanity both physical life and spiritual death. It is this seed of sin inherent in human nature that causes us to resist God's will and His voice. It is only through God's prevenient grace that we can be rescued from this spiritual death.

Those who earnestly seek God discover that, by practicing the spiritual disciplines, their relationship with the Lord thrives, and as that relationship thrives, it becomes easier to understand and follow God's will. The title of a Christian classic written by A. W. Tozer, *The Pursuit of God,* illustrates this principle. When we intentionally set out to discover more about God and pursue a deepening relationship with Him, we discover that through grace our resistance begins to subside, and it becomes easier to hear His voice and follow His will. A good way to experience an increase in the inflow of God's grace is by faithfully pursuing God through the spiritual disciplines.

These practices increase our strength to resist evil and submit to Christ's lordship. They heighten our desire for Him and invite Him to have an increasing influence over our lives. There are five basic spiritual disciplines discussed below to help the Christian sojourner discern God's will. They include attending worship services, reading and studying the scriptures, prayer, fasting, and meditation.

Worship Attendance

While it is assumed that most people who are considering entering the ministry regularly attend a church, that is not always the case. Some do not regularly attend church while studying for the ministry. They reason they will wait until they are ready for the licensure process to begin before they begin faithfully attending church. This is unfortunate. What they fail to realize is that they are cutting off a vital avenue of how God's grace flows into our lives.

Intermittent church attendance robs people of the spiritual benefits that come with regularly fellowshipping with other believers, hearing the Word preached, blending our voices in the hymns of praise and worship, partaking in the Lord's Supper, and a host of similar activities. The spiritual benefits that come from regular church attendance are too numerous to list. It goes without saying that if a person expects to be a spiritual leader in the church, they should have considerable experience of regularly worshipping with fellow believers and experiencing the benefits of regular church attendance.

Scripture

In addition to church attendance, a second spiritual discipline is regularly reading and studying the Bible. During a recent spring semester, midway through a course in the Gospels, I became concerned that my students were not grasping how the scriptures were alive with the Spirit of God speaking directly into our lives. My students were putting in just enough effort to pass the tests and get a decent grade in the course.

More out of frustration than skill as a professor, I challenged them to experiment over the weekend by devoting thirty minutes a day for five days and doing nothing but quietly reading the Bible and meditating on what they were reading. They were instructed to find a quiet place, turn off their cell phones, turn off all music, unless it was soft background music, turn off the TV, and eliminate any other distractions and spend thirty minutes a day quietly reading the Bible and listening to the voice of the Spirit as they read. At the end of the experiment, they were to report back what happened.

By the next week, I had forgotten that I had given them the challenge. However, at the beginning of class, one student interrupted me and asked if he could share what happened when he tried the experiment. He told the class that, during his life, he had struggled with depression and thoughts of suicide. However, that weekend while reading the Bible, he experienced such inner calmness and peace that he had never before experienced in his life. He discovered the Bible was alive with God's voice speaking into his life.

Another student immediately held up his Bible with page after page highlighted. He told the class that the scriptures were so alive that he found it hard to put his Bible down. He just kept highlighting page after page because the Bible was speaking powerfully to him. Another student across the aisle quickly added that she, too, had a similar experience. As a professor, I was thrilled to see my students had learned more through that simple activity than perhaps all the other activities in class. They discovered that when we give the Spirit a chance to speak to us through the scriptures, He speaks powerfully. His word is "Alive and active. Sharper than any double-edged sword, it penetrates even to dividing soul and spirit, joints and marrow; it judges the thoughts and attitudes of the heart" (Hebrews 4:12 NIV).

There is no other book in the world that is filled with so much guidance as the Bible if we take the time to study it. Most of the direction we need in life can be found within its pages. It has been estimated that over 90 percent of the answers to all the questions we have about life can be found in the Bible. The Bible gives us explicit direction about basic moral principles, such as telling the truth and not lying, working and not stealing, how to treat our parents and neighbors, and practicing sexual integrity. In the Bible, we find direct answers to many of life's issues.

The more we know about the Bible, the better equipped we are to make good decisions in life and to communicate the Word of God. Scriptural knowledge equips us with the truth. When we face moral issues, they give clear guidance. Our Creator, who built into the created order His eternal principles, has given us the scriptures to teach us the ways of God. As Christians, the Bible is our final authority for faith and practice.

Some safeguards should be used to ensure that we properly understand what is written in the Bible. A haphazard or illogical approach to reading the Bible can lead to error. For example, when we say a short prayer asking God to guide us to the right verse and then randomly open the Bible and blindly place our finger on a particular verse, trusting this text to be God's answer to our question, we will likely twist the scriptures to say something that God never intended for them to say. One person using this method opened the Bible and placed his finger on a verse that read "Judas went out and hanged himself." That passage did not give him the satisfaction he sought, so he flipped a few pages and did the same thing again. This time the verse read, "Go and do thou likewise." The Lord does not work in that manner.

The method used by evangelical Christians is called the historical-grammatical method of interpretation. This method seeks to first know the historical context of the author when the document was written. What was his setting? What was the situation of the people to whom he was writing? What did the people who were the first to read the letter understand it to mean? A study Bible helps provide background information for each book of the Bible.

Students should experiment with different methods of reading and studying the Bible to discover which practices benefit them the most. Robert Mulholland lists two methods to be used in reading the scriptures. The first is to read the scriptures for information. Using this method, the reader seeks to garner as much information as possible from reading the text. The more biblical information that is fixed in our minds, the better we assimilate that information into our thinking.

A second way is to read the Bible in a formational manner. This requires the reader to slow down and allow the Spirit to speak to them as they read the text. The reader reads slowly and from time to time goes back to previous paragraphs or verses and rereads them to gain greater clarity (Mulholland 2001).

A third way is to memorize scripture. Memorizing scripture enables the person to store away the scripture in their minds. Before the summer break, I challenge students to memorize the Sermon on the Mount. If they commit to memory that sermon, they have a little preacher with them all summer long that helps them to make good decisions. Dallas Willard wrote, "As a pastor, teacher, and counselor I have repeatedly seen the transformation of inner and outer life that comes simply from the memorization and meditation upon Scripture" (Dallas Willard 2010).

Prayer

A third spiritual discipline is prayer. From the beginning of time, people have sought to connect with their Creator through prayer. After the flood, Noah built an altar and offered a sacrifice to God. When Abraham arrived in Palestine, he built an altar and worshiped God. Later, whenever he settled, he built altars. His sons Isaac and Jacob built altars. When God established His covenant with the Israelites at Sinai, He gave them the pattern for the Tabernacle and later temple. That was the place where they came to meet with God. In the New Testament, when Jesus observed people using the temple as a place of commerce, He quoted Isaiah, pointing out the central purpose for the sanctuary was for prayer. He said, "It is written, 'My house will be called a house of prayer" (Matthew 21:13 NIV).

For us to know God's will, we must spend time communicating with Him and building relationships with Him. Jesus taught that a good way to pray is to get alone, close the door to outside distractions, and talk with our heavenly Father alone. "When you pray, go into your room, close the door and pray to your Father, who is unseen. Then your Father, who sees what is done in secret, will reward you" (Matthew 6:6 NIV). He did not exclude public prayer by this teaching. Public prayer is important but does not have the same spiritual impact as private prayer.

Prayer is incredibly powerful. James referred to the story of Elijah in Israel during the time of King Ahab and wrote, "Elijah was a human being, even as we are. He prayed earnestly that it would not rain, and it did not rain on the land for three and a half years. Again, he prayed, and the heavens gave rain, and the earth produced its crops" (James 5:17 NIV). There are many other stories throughout the Bible of how the Lord answered the prayers of His servants in powerful ways.

The more time we spend in prayer, the easier it becomes to hear God's voice and accept His will for our lives. The Hebrew writer says, "Let us, therefore, come boldly unto the throne of grace, that we may obtain mercy and find grace to help in time of need" (Hebrews 4:16 KJV). Dallas Willard wrote:

> Indeed, the indirect effects of prayer upon the conduct of our lives are so obvious and striking that they have mistakenly been treated at times as the only point of prayer. Even when we are praying for or about things other than our own spiritual needs and growth, the effect of conversing with God cannot fail to have a pervasive and spiritually strengthening effect on all aspects of our personality. (Dallas Willard 2010)

I challenge people who come to me for counsel about their needs and concerns to write a short prayer requesting the Lord's help and to regularly lift that prayer to the Lord. Over time, that prayer will become memorized as they allow the Spirit to lead them to make small, nuanced changes to their requests. This process aligns their requests with God's will. If they keep a prayer journal, it makes it easy to go back and see how the Lord has answered their prayers.

Fasting

A fourth spiritual discipline that helps a person understand God's special call is fasting. Fasting is closely associated with prayer. When we fast, we deny our physical body its natural appetites to focus our minds and spirits on the voice of the Spirit. After His baptism, Jesus spent forty days fasting. At the end of His forty-day fast, Christ was tempted by Satan but was strong in the face of temptation. Moses fasted forty days both times he was on Mount Sinai in God's presence receiving the Ten Commandments.

In the New Testament, after Jesus's ascension, the disciples at Antioch were fasting and praying when the Spirit led them to commission Barnabas and Paul for their first missionary journey to Cyprus and Asia Minor. (See Acts 13:2.) Paul and Barnabas prayed and fasted before they chose elders and leaders in the churches they had founded on that missionary journey.

Jesus instructed us about our attitudes when we fast. We are not to make a display of it but seek to keep it between ourselves and the Lord. We should seek to disguise the fact we are fasting with a shower and a fresh smell. "When you fast, do not look somber as the hypocrites do, for they disfigure their faces to show others they are fasting. Truly I tell you, they have received their reward in full. But when you fast, put oil on your head and wash your face, so that it will not be obvious to others that you are fasting, but only to your Father, who is unseen; and your Father, who sees what is done in secret, will reward you" (Matthew 6:16–18 NIV).

Fasting makes it easier to understand God's will and bolsters our courage to follow His leading. John Stott pointed out that, when the topic of fasting was brought up, Jesus expected that His disciples would fast. Jesus said, "When you fast." The Bible teaches that fasting is not to be an isolated practice and that it is associated with penitence, self-discipline, concern for the hungry, and special times of prayer (Stott, The Radical Disciple 2010). In the New Testament, within the practice of Judaism, Jews fasted twice each week. In the early days of Methodism, John Wesley encouraged his people to practice fasting two meals each week.

Bill Bright, the founder of Campus Crusade (now CRU), felt impressed to go on a forty-day fast to seek revival for the nation. He outlined seven steps to follow when planning an extended fast. These steps are:

First, set a specific objective for your fast.
Second, prepare yourself spiritually.
Third, prepare yourself physically.
Fourth, ask the Holy Spirit to reveal the kind of fast he
wants you to undertake.
Fifth, limit your activity level.
Sixth, consider your medications.

Seventh, set aside ample time to be alone with the Lord (Bright, Seven Basic Steps to Successful Fasting and Prayer 2009).

Meditation

A fifth spiritual discipline that helps us clarify God's will for our lives is meditation. This is not an Eastern meditation that is a part of mysticism. Rather, it is the practice of mulling over in our minds the Word of God— often a passage of scripture. It enables us to filter out all the noise and distractions of the world and listen for the voice of the Spirit. It is beneficial to have a copy of the Bible before us as we meditate and reflect on various passages from the scriptures.

This often helps us clarify the meaning of a particular passage of scripture and probe deeper into its meaning. In our world of twenty-four-seven information and distractions, it is often difficult to find time to be alone with God for an extended time. However, when we intentionally set aside time to meditate by shutting off outside distractions to listen to the voice of the Spirit, we discover we are spiritually nourished.

It is helpful to engage in a spiritual retreat from time to time. One of my seminary professors shared his experience of taking annual spiritual retreats while completing his doctorate. He set aside two weeks each year for a spiritual retreat. He observed that by the third day of his retreat, he was hearing things from God that he had been unable to hear on the first day. By the end of two weeks, he was hearing things from the Spirit that he had been unable to hear on the third day. The Lord promised the Israelites facing Babylonian captivity, "You will seek me and find me when you seek me with all your heart" (Jeremiah 29:13 NIV).

The more earnestly we seek the Lord's leadership and guidance for our lives by engaging in the spiritual disciplines, the stronger our faith becomes and the easier it becomes for us to discern God's will. Finding the will of God for our lives sometimes comes down to the matter of our resolve. Are we willing to humble ourselves before Him, submit to His lordship, and seek Him earnestly with all our hearts? Practicing the spiritual disciplines is an effective way to overcome inner resistance and embrace God's calling for our lives. We will now turn to the clergy/laity debate.

Questions

1. What are the two primary meanings of the expression *the will of God*?
2. Describe Timothy's call into the ministry.
3. Describe Luke's motivation to write his Gospel and Acts.
4. What are the spiritual disciplines?
5. How does practicing the spiritual disciplines help to clarify the call to the ministry?
6. How often do you read the Bible?
7. Experiment with journaling your prayers for one month.
8. List Bill Bright's seven steps to fasting.
9. Have you experimented with fasting?

Bright, B. 1995. *The Coming Revival.* Orlando: New Life Publications.

Bright, B. 2009. *Seven Basic Steps to Successful Fasting and Prayer.* Peachtree, GA: Campus Crusade for Christ.

Dallas Willard. 2010. *A Place for Truth.* Downers Grove, IL: InterVarsity Press.

Mulholland, R. 2001. Shaped by the Word: The Power of Scripture in Spiritual Formation: Upper Room Books

Smith, M. B. 1991. *Knowing God's Will.* Downers Grove, IL: InterVarsity Press.

Stott, J. 2010. *The Radical Disciple.* Nottingham, England: InterVarsity Press.

God's Anointed

Do not touch My anointed ones; do my prophets no harm.
—Psalm 16:22 (NIV)

The Messiah was the name the Jews used to describe the person whom they hoped would come and free them from their oppressors. That is an interesting title for the person whom they expected would be a warrior king and once again establish their nation. They believed he would be anointed with God's favor and blessing and liberate them from their oppressors. However, the Messiah whom God sent to them was the Prince of Peace. Sometimes we get it wrong with our predictions.

The word *messiah* is simply a transliteration of the Hebrew word for the a*nointed one*. The Greek word for *messiah* is *christ*. Where did the idea of an anointed one originate in Jewish culture?

The first occasion in the Bible of a person being anointed for his work was Aaron and his sons when they were installed as priests in Israel. Special anointing oil was used to consecrate them for their work. The anointing ceremony symbolized that God was setting them apart for His service and ordaining them for their work in Tabernacle worship. The anointing ceremony was called ordination.

God chose Aaron to be Israel's first high priest and his family line to continue the succession of priests. At Sinai, when Kohath and other members of this Levite clan attempted to usurp Aaron's priestly role, the Lord caused the earth to open and swallow the insurgents and their families. (See Numbers 16.) Not just anyone was authorized to stand before the Lord and lead the people in worship. It is God's prerogative to choose whom He wills for leadership roles in His kingdom.

Anointing oil was used for more than just anointing priests for their work. The prophet Samuel was sent to anoint Saul, Israel's first king, first in a ceremony near Samuel's home. Later, he assembled the leaders of Israel for the formal anointing ceremony of Saul. Several years later, he was sent to Jesse's house to anoint David as Israel's second king. Later, when Solomon was installed as Israel's third king, he too was anointed with oil in a formal ceremony. This anointing indicated God's favor and blessing would be upon the person as they carried out their responsibilities of leading Israel.

Throughout the Bible, there are other examples of people being anointed for their work with formal and informal ceremonies. However, in contrast to the priests and kings, the prophets for the most part did not have a formal anointing ceremony initiating them into their ministry. From the time of their encounter with God, these men and women lived with the knowledge that God's call was upon them, and they felt responsible to faithfully preach His Word to the people.

When Jesus began His ministry, he was baptized with water by His cousin John the Baptist in the Jordan River. On that occasion, there was a supernatural display of God's anointing upon Jesus when the Holy Spirit descended upon Him in the form of a dove.

Later, when He returned to His hometown of Nazareth, in the

synagogue on the Sabbath with the people gathered for worship, He read to them from the scroll of Isaiah and proclaimed, "The Spirit of the Lord is on me because he has anointed me to proclaim good news to the poor" (Luke 4:18 NIV). Jesus's entire ministry was under the leadership of two other members of the Trinity: the Father and the Holy Spirit.

It was well into His ministry before His disciples fully realized that He was the Anointed One. Toward the middle of His ministry, Jesus asked His disciples who they thought He was. Peter responded by repeating what people were saying about him: some saying He was John the Baptist raised from the dead, Elijah, Jeremiah, or one of the prophets. But Jesus asked the disciples specifically, "'But what about you?' he asked. 'Who do you say I am?'" (Mark 8:29 NIV). In a moment of inspiration, Peter exclaimed, "You are the Messiah" (Mark 8:29 NIV). This was an incredibly enlightening moment for Peter and the other disciples when it dawned upon them that Jesus was their long-awaited Messiah.

The Special Call

The idea of a special call from God for the work of ministry is anchored in the belief the Lord specifically calls some people to dedicate their lives to the ministry and anoints them for their work. Further, the church is given the authority to recognize those who are called and commission them for the work. However, some question this process. They believe that much of the ministry that is done exclusively by clergy is out of step with the New Testament. They question if perhaps the ordination process is a creation by the church and misses God's highest purpose for His body. In some instances, it may even impede the Lord's work rather than advance it. This may raise the question about the people who testify to having the Lord's special call to ministry if perhaps it is a personal ambition rather than God's call. Did they misunderstand the Lord's voice? After all, is the ordination process a human invention or a practice anchored in the scriptures?

Paul Stevens raises this question in his book *The Other Six Days* (Stevens 1999, Stevens 1999). George Barna and Frank Viola ask similar questions and point out that several of the church's historic practices were borrowed from secular and pagan organizations (Frank Viola, George Barna 2008). They ask if perhaps the church missed the mark when it began ordaining clergy.

Barna and Viola point out, "The word pastor does not appear in the New Testament." In Ephesians 4:11, where it does appear, they comment, "At best Ephesians 4:11 is oblique" (Frank Viola, George Barna 2008). Their line of reasoning is that every Christian is called to minister, and ordaining a select class of clergy tends to blur that mandate.

Indeed, all Christians are called to minister full-time. God does not redeem us to be reservoirs of His grace and hoard His blessings. God is a giving person, and as His image bearers, we are created to be conduits, allowing His grace to flow out of our lives, leaving this world a better place than we found it. That raises the question, "Does the Lord call some believers to dedicate their lives and careers primarily to ministry, or are all believers called alike to be engaged in the ministry of building God's kingdom?" To answer this question, we begin in the Old Testament and trace religious leadership throughout the Bible to see how the Lord called people to their roles.

Old Testament Worship

From Sinai throughout the end of the Old Testament, much of Israel's formal worship took place at the Tabernacle and later temples. Worshippers brought their sacrifices to the priests to be offered on the altar that stood in front of the Tabernacle and Temple. This practice continued until the Babylonian captivity when the First Temple was destroyed, and temple worship ceased.

Worship at the Second Temple was later resumed when it was rebuilt by groups of Jews who were permitted to return to Jerusalem and rebuild their Temple. Worship at the Second Temple continued through the time of Christ, except for a brief interruption when Antiochus Epiphanes profaned the Temple with pagan worship. The Temple was later purged, and worship restored by the Maccabees. However, it ceased altogether in AD 70 when the Romans leveled Herod's Temple and razed the city. Following the destruction of Jerusalem, the people were forced to worship exclusively in synagogues. Within a few decades of the destruction of Herod's Temple, the exclusive class of Jewish priests ceased to exist. This happened because the activities of the priests centered on temple worship and were no longer possible when their temple was destroyed.

Synagogues most likely began during the Babylonian captivity when it was not possible to worship at a temple in Jerusalem. The Jews began gathering in synagogues and eventually brought this practice back to Palestine. Over time, the synagogues became the religious hub of Jewish communities. While Temple worship required animal sacrifices and was led exclusively by priests, worship in the synagogue was led by local leaders and included the reading of the scriptures and prayers. While the Torah specifies how priests are to be selected for Temple worship, there are no specifications in the Bible about how leaders are chosen for the synagogue. Synagogues are not mentioned in the Old Testament.

By the time of Christ, synagogues had become an integral part of Jewish communities, with many synagogues being located in Palestine— several hundred were located in the Jerusalem area alone. Following His baptism, Jesus returned to Nazareth to worship at the local synagogue. Later, when He made Capernaum the home base for ministry, He regularly worshipped in the synagogue located there.

A couple of observations should be noted about synagogue worship in contrast to temple worship. First, the Temple was supervised by the priests, while the synagogues were supervised by local leaders. By the time of Christ, more priests lived in the vicinity of Jerusalem than could serve a Temple rotation. Consequently, priests were selected by a lottery system for the privilege of serving in the Temple.

Second, synagogues did not have an altar for animal sacrifices as did the Temple. Worship in the synagogues included prayer and the reading of the scriptures. The experts of the Law tended to gather in Jerusalem around the Temple and to a lesser extent around the synagogues.

Third, synagogues were located near where the people lived, while the Temple was in Jerusalem. Having a synagogue nearby allowed people to regularly gather to worship each Sabbath. In contrast, worshiping at the Temple required worshippers to make pilgrimages to Jerusalem. Who were the people who provided spiritual leadership in Israel?

The Priests

On Sinai, God specifically directed Moses to appoint Aaron as the high priest of Israel, and upon his death, the succession of priests was to follow his family line. They were from the tribe of Levi and charged with the responsibility of overseeing worship at the Tabernacle and religious activities throughout the nation. The Levite clan was called to assist the priests with the care of the Tabernacle, its worship functions, and other religious functions in outlying areas.

By the end of Judges, Eli was the high priest in charge of the Tabernacle and its worship when it was located at Shiloh. However, his sons were greedy and immoral and sought to integrate the idolatrous practices of the surrounding Canaanite nations into worship at the Tabernacle. In Israel, it was a time of spiritual darkness and moral decline. God brought judgment on Eli's house and family by allowing Eli to die of heart failure and his sons to die on the battlefield when the Ark of the Covenant was captured by the Philistines. It was during this period that the Lord spoke to the prophet Samuel and called him to serve as a priest, a prophet, and a judge.

Priests continued to serve the Tabernacle and later temples throughout the Old Testament. They served at Solomon's Temple until the time of its destruction by the Babylonians. When the Second Temple was rebuilt, the line of the priests returned to serve through the time of Christ.

Priests in New Testament Times

By the time of Christ, the function of priests in Temple worship was under the political control of the Romans. At Jesus's crucifixion, Caiaphas, the son-in-law of Annas, was the high priest who was recognized by the Romans. However, Annas, his father-in-law, was considered the legitimate high priest by the Jews. At Jesus's trial, He was first taken to Annas and judged by the Jews, then sent to Caiaphas, who was the person authorized to send Him to Pilate. (See John 18:13–24.) Annas did not have the authority to send Christ to Governor Pilate to be executed.

Scribes

During the Babylonian captivity, another group of influential religious leaders emerged—the scribes. One of the most influential of these spiritual leaders was Ezra. He was both a priest and a scribe. However, his role as a scribe appears to supersede his role as a priest. Many scholars consider Ezra to be second only to Moses as far as spiritual stature and influence over Israel. Under the leadership of the governor Nehemiah, a platform was built for Ezra to publicly read the Law. (See Nehemiah 8.) On that occasion, Levites were placed throughout the congregation to help the people understand what was being read as Ezra read the Torah.

This story indicates how the role of scribes had an increasing influence on the religious life of the Jews after the Babylonian captivity. Perhaps this role was driven by the need to copy the scriptures for synagogue worship. In Babylon, when the people were no longer able to worship at the Temple in Jerusalem, they turned to gather in synagogues where the scriptures were publicly read to them. By the time of Christ, the public reading of the scriptures was an integral part of synagogue worship.

The Prophets

Another group of spiritual leaders in the Old Testament who wielded an increasingly significant influence in the spiritual life of the Israelites was the prophets. They were God's spokesmen and spokeswomen who were individually called by God to communicate His Word to the leaders and their people. Chuck Colson emphasized this role with the title of one of his books, *Who Speaks for God?* (Colson 1994).

The prophets were charged with standing before the leaders and their people in the place of God to deliver His Word to them. In that role, they share much in common with the preacher today. Preachers are not called to preach their opinions and notions but to faithfully communicate God's Word to the people.

In contrast to the priests, the prophets did not come into their roles because of their family line or heritage. Rather, they were individually called by God. While the expression "the sons of the prophets" appears in the Bible, it refers to a group of prophets living and studying in small religious communities and is variously translated as "the company of the prophets," "the guild of prophets," "the group of prophets," and "disciples of prophets." (See 1 Kings 20:35; 2 Kings 2:3, 5, 7, 15; 4:1, 38; 5:22; 6:1; and Amos 2:11.) This expression does not necessarily mean that their biological fathers were prophets, as was the case of priests.

Most Old Testament scholars agree the era of prophets began with the preaching of Elijah. Although other leaders before him are referred to as prophets, such as Abraham, Moses, Miriam (Moses's sister), Deborah, and Samuel, the golden age of the prophets began with the preaching of Elijah and Elisha and continued through the exile and beyond to the end of the Old Testament. John the Baptist was the last of the prophets.

Some of the prophets wrote down their messages, and these messages are included in the Bible under their names, such as Isaiah, Jeremiah, and Joel. They are referred to as the writing prophets. However, neither Elijah nor Elisha is among the writing prophets. Their stories are embedded in the books Kings and Chronicles.

Elijah does not tell how he was called to his work. He simply emerges in Israel during the reign of King Ahab, denounces Baal worship, and announces there would be no rain in the land until the Lord sent him with the word that rain was coming again.

For the next three years, there was no rain on the land. At the end of that period, he appeared again to announce that rain was coming and held a contest with the prophets of Baal on Mount Carmel. Sacrifices were prepared by both the prophets of Baal and Elijah and the God who answered by fire was the true God of Israel. On that occasion, the prophets of Baal prayed all day long, even cutting themselves, with nothing happening. This was followed by a simple prayer by Elijah when the Lord answered in a fire that consumed both the sacrifice and altar. (See 1 Kings 18.) That event was followed by a rainstorm that swept across the land.

Prophets were called from all walks of life and were often busy in their vocational work when the Lord called them. Following Elijah's experience on Mount Carmel, he was sent to anoint Elisha as his successor. When Elijah arrived at his home, Elisha was in the field plowing. Elijah threw his outer garment over Elisha, indicating that he was to be Elijah's apprentice and successor. Elisha's response was to use the plowing instruments for firewood and sacrifice the oxen. He was committed to following God's call.

New Testament Worship

As noted above, during the time of Christ, most worship in Palestine took place in two primary places—the Temple and the synagogues. The only story about Jesus's boyhood recorded in the New Testament took place in the Temple at the Passover Feast. Jesus was engaged in conversation with the religious experts and failed to realize his parents had left town to return to Nazareth.

When Jesus went to Jerusalem for the feasts, He would worship at Herod's Temple, where He often encountered religious teachers. These teachers gathered in the Temple area to discuss the scriptures and engage student learners in conversations about the Jewish religion, its traditions, and its customs. In the Temple area, Jesus taught his disciples and ministered by healing the sick. He also carried out these ministries in the villages and towns throughout Galilee, Samaria, and the surrounding area.

Paul worshiped in the Temple at Jerusalem before and after his conversion. Following his third missionary journey, after being away from Jerusalem for several years, Paul made a special pilgrimage to Jerusalem to worship at the Temple. On that occasion, he was arrested in the Temple compound and spent nearly four years of incarceration in Palestine and Rome. (See Acts 20:13–28:31.)

In the first years of the church, Christians initially sought to worship with the Jews in the Temple and their synagogues but were soon forced out. Despite this resistance, it was Paul's custom on his missionary journeys when he first entered a town or city to go to the local synagogue. After they were forced out of the synagogues, Christians began meeting in their homes, and house churches became the primary gathering place for Christians during the first centuries of the church.

During those early decades in the formation of the church's organization, much of its organization was modeled after the synagogues. On their first missionary journey, after planting churches in Asia Minor, Paul and Barnabas on their return journey to Antioch revisited the towns and appointed elders to oversee the congregations. No doubt the selection of the local leadership was modeled after the synagogues. (See Acts 14:23.)

As a result, not many details of church organizations are prescribed in the Bible. Under the leadership of the Holy Spirit, they did what was prudent to preserve their work. As the church grew and required more organization, new leadership patterns began to emerge in the church. However, much of this took place after the New Testament was written.

In the early centuries of the church, there were several significant developments. First, there was the phenomenal growth of Christianity. It quickly spread from Palestine to Asia Minor, to Europe, to Africa, around the Mediterranean Sea, and in other parts of the world. Second, some of the cardinal doctrines of the Christian faith were formulated, including establishing the New Testament canon of scriptures, formulating the doctrine of Christ's deity, the deity of the Holy Spirit, and the Trinity. The deliberation of these and similar doctrines was only possible because of the church's ecclesiastical organization. The leadership was able to protect the body from heresy and hammer out some of its cardinal doctrines because it was organized to the level it was. The leaders in this deliberative process were for the most part people who today we would identify as clergy.

New Testament Church Organization

It was not until after the New Testament was written that the process of recognizing and ordaining church leaders developed into a formal process. As a result, today there is variation among Christian denominations in their ordination practices.

In his letters to Timothy and Titus, Paul includes a list of character traits for church leaders but does not specify how they were to be selected; nor does he say that just because a person possesses these qualities, they are automatically qualified for church leadership roles. (See 1 Timothy 3:1–10 and Titus 1:5–9.)

Because the selection of church leaders was in its early stages of development when the New Testament was written, some question whether the church missed the mark when it began ordaining a special class of church leaders called clergy. They point to the fact that in the first century, two categories of believers did not exist. They believe identifying and ordaining clergy as the church's leaders causes an unnecessary division within the church, resulting in two categories of believers: clergy and laity. Clergy are perceived as those who are the spiritually elite, while the laity is often regarded as second-class Christians. In the New Testament, except for the apostles, all believers were considered equal members of the body.

It is important to keep our practices aligned with scripture and in harmony with the leadership of the Spirit, especially when it comes to placing people in ministry. It is God's prerogative who He calls into the ministry. Jesus told the twelve, "I have chosen you out of the world" (John 15:19 NIV). While the church does not have the prerogative of calling whoever it wishes into the ministry, it does have the responsibility of recognizing and affirming those whom God has called.

A few years ago, while participating in a series of conferences to revise and update our denomination's clergy ordination requirements, an inquiry was made about the average age of ordination candidates. The initial response of one of the church statisticians was that the age of ordinands had changed very little from previous decades. When he was asked to double-check the statistics, he came back surprised and commented that the average age had increased almost three years during the most recent decade. What appeared to be happening was an increasing number of middle-aged, second-career adults were seeking ordination. God was at work calling them into the ministry, and the church had not caught up with that change. The church's ordination process must be flexible enough to accommodate how God works to call people into the ministry.

Challenges of the Language Used

Those who question the practice of ordination typically point to the problem of distinguishing between the ministry done by clergy and that done by the laity. There is often little difference between the two because the words *minister* and *ministry* can equally be used about most of the work done by both clergy and laity.

Os Guinness points out that it is difficult to define precisely what is meant by *full-time Christian service* or *full-time ministry*. He contends that all Christians are called to serve the Lord full-time. Also, many times it is impossible to separate the ministry done by ministers from that done by the laity (Guinness 1998). His line of reasoning is that all believers are called to continually minister, and the practice of ordaining a select group of leaders brings an unhealthy division within the body.

A problem also arises when pastors challenge parishioners to engage in ministry and to not rely on the pastoral staff to do all the work of the church. What ministry is only done by the clergy? What separates the ministry done by clergy from that done by the laity? It is often assumed the pastor primarily delivers the sermons and leads the ceremonial functions of the church, such as communion, funerals, baptisms, and so on. But there are no specific guidelines about this in the Bible. Indeed, Paul, who was one of the most prolific evangelists in the New Testament, wrote that it was not his custom to baptize believers. (See 1 Corinthians 1:17.)

The Special Call

The idea of a special call from God is anchored in God's call for some people to dedicate their careers to vocational ministry. Further, the church is given the authority to recognize those who are called and commission them for their work. However, if this assumption is invalid and the ordination process is an invention of the church, then the practice of ordination may be out of step with God's highest purpose for the church and in some instances may even hinder the Lord's work rather than enhance it. Does the ordination process reflect a human invention rather than a practice anchored in the scriptures?

During the first century, when the New Testament was being written, neither the words *clergy* nor *laity* were used in the New Testament. It was not until years later that their usage emerged in the church and they took on distinctive meanings. In the second, third, and fourth centuries, as the church grew and became more formally organized, it began to identify its leaders as clergy.

The Greek word for clergy, *klerikos*, originally meant *a lot* (Webster 1996) or "portion assigned to someone" (Stevens 1999). In the New Testament, this word was used to describe the process in which the soldiers got a particular item of Jesus's clothing at his crucifixion. They cast lots for His clothing. It is also used to describe how the eleven apostles chose Matthias as Judas's successor.

The word *laity* comes from the Greek word *laos* and means "a crowd of people." It is used in the Septuagint (the Greek translation of the Hebrew Old Testament) to refer to the *people of God*. Arndt and Gringrich describe it as being "the people in contrast to the Pharisees and legal experts ... the people in contrast to the priests" (William Arndt, Wilbur Gringrich 1957).

In the New Testament, neither of these words had the religious connotations they have today. It was not until the end of the first century that Clement of Rome used *laos* to refer to the general body of Christians as distinct from church leaders (Stevens 1999).

At about the same time, Ignatius used the title *bishop* to identify leaders over a group of churches in a particular region (Frank Viola, George Barna 2008). As pointed out earlier, most scholars agree that in the New Testament, the words translated *bishop*, *elder*, and *overseer* are used interchangeably. The title of *elder* was a carryover from the Jewish communities and has remained pretty much the same over the centuries. The words *bishop* and *overseer* are translations of similar Greek words and were used in secular settings to identify leaders.

By the fourth century, when the church began constructing cathedrals and moving away from house churches and buildings and property became more of an issue, these words took on a more distinctive meaning. In addition to identifying spiritual leaders, they were used to identify those who oversaw its buildings and identified them as clergy.

Over the centuries, a subtle change took place with the usage of the word *laity*. It took on its Old Testament meaning in the Septuagint as the people of God and began to be the people as separate from the clergy. In the Middle Ages, it morphed into the idea that laity needed clergy to be their spiritual intermediaries. This error, in part, contributed to the Protestant Reformation, leading Martin Luther to advocate the priesthood of all believers. He taught that all Christians, regardless of their titles or positions, are members of the priesthood of believers and do not need an intermediary to intercede for them. Each believer stands on an equal footing before God.

However, except for some groups such as the Anabaptists, the second generation of reformers was not as enthusiastic about Luther's teaching about the priesthood of all believers. The reformers continued the ordination process as it had been practiced for centuries.

The Prophet/Preacher

In the New Testament, *prophets* are mentioned less frequently than in the second half of the Old Testament, with Luke only using this word four times in Acts. In those instances, the prophets foretold impending disasters. (See Acts 11:27, 13:1, 15:32, and 21:10.) Although Paul uses the title of the prophet in his letters to Corinth and Ephesus, prophets are not mentioned as frequently in the New Testament. (See 1 Corinthians 12: 28 and 14:29.) After the first century, this office does not appear to have widespread usages like that of elder, bishop, and deacon.

While the title of the prophet may not have persisted in the church over the centuries, the role of the prophet did; it is perhaps more like the role of the preacher today than is that of the priest, especially within evangelical Christianity. While the title *priest* is used in some denominations to refer to clergy, most Protestant churches have chosen to use other titles.

There are several reasons that prophets serve as better role models for preachers today than does the title *priest*. First, prophets were individually called by God to their ministry. That is also true of most preachers. Those who are being ordained are expected to testify about a call from God that qualifies them for ministry.

Second, pastors—like prophets—come from all walks of life. Amos was busy with his ranching and farming in Tekoah when the Lord called him. (See Amos 7:14.) Although he was from Judah, the Lord sent him to the neighboring nation of Israel to deliver God's message to the king. When one of the priests from Bethel ordered Amos to leave the country, he responded, "I was neither a prophet nor the son of a prophet, but I was a shepherd, and I also took care of sycamore-fig trees. But the Lord took me from tending the flock and said to me, 'Go, prophesy to my people Israel'" (Amos 7:14–15 NIV). Jeremiah was from the priestly clan. Isaiah was probably from the royal clan. In contrast to the individual call of the prophet, the priests came solely from the Levites.

Third, the prophets' ministry focused on communicating God's Word to the people, while the priests' ministry was focused on the ceremonial functions of worship. The priests oversaw the sacrificial offerings at the altar and attended to the maintenance of the Tabernacle and temples. The prophets received messages from the Lord and were responsible for faithfully communicating those messages to the people. Priests learned about the ceremonial practices through their training in the Temple. Prophets were called to preach the Word of God and were forbidden to preach their ideas.

In using the title of the priest for its pastors, the Roman Catholic Church and similar mainline denominations that use the title priest for its clergy emphasize that the primary function of clergy roles is leading the ceremonial functions of worship, in contrast to the preaching of the Word. It is to be noted that the Roman Catholic Church has seven sacraments exclusively administered by priests, in contrast to most Protestant churches that have only two: communion and baptism. Instead of focusing on the administration of the sacraments, Protestantism has placed more emphasis on the proclamation of the Word.

Fourth, the prophets did not have a guaranteed source of income as did the priests. The priests were given allotted portions from the tithes and offerings of the people. In contrast, the prophets had no guarantees of income other than the assurance that the one who called them would be faithful to take care of them. Elisha was sustained at first by a brook of water and ravens. When the brook dried up, he was sent to Zarephath in Sidon where a widow lived with her son. She was on the verge of starvation when Elisha arrived. However, when she followed Elisha's instructions, she saw her last bit of meal and oil miraculously sustained through the end of the drought.

This is not to suggest that preachers and pastors should not be supported by their congregations. Indeed, Paul teaches that those who minister have a legitimate right to receive a portion of the tithes and offerings brought by the people. (See 1 Corinthians 9:14.) However, it is to suggest that the primary motivation for ministry for those who are ordained is because of God's call and not a random vocational choice.

This does not mean that bivocational pastors who are gainfully employed in other vocations are not faithfully answering their call. Paul was a bivocational missionary, often using his tent-making skills to support both his ministry and those who traveled with him.

Fifth, the Bible teaches the priesthood of all believers. This was one of Martin Luther's strong points about how the church should regard the body of Christ—clergy should not be regarded as the spiritually elite while laity should be regarded of lesser spiritual quality. Additionally, Christians do not need an intermediary to intercede for them. Each believer can go directly to Christ. The scriptures teach the priesthood of all believers. (See Hebrews 8:8-12.) "But you are a chosen people, a royal priesthood, a holy nation, God's special possession, that you may declare the praises of him who called you out of darkness into his wonderful light" (1 Peter 2:9 NIV). For these reasons and others, the title *priest* does not seem to be the best title to use for the Protestant pastor today.

John Stott says that a revival has never happened that was not first preceded by a revival of preaching (Stott, The Radical Disciple 2010)[1]. That was the case in the Old Testament. When the people drifted away from God, got into trouble, and turned to God for help, He answered their prayers by sending one of His prophets.

Those who advocate eliminating the designation of a special class of church leaders as *clergy* to eliminate confusion about who does what ministry tend to overlook the special call of God. It seems that God has honored the way the church identifies and appoints its leaders. God continues to call His servants to dedicate their lives to the work of ministry through a special calling and anoints them for this work.

Through the divine election, God chooses whom He wills to fill the leadership roles in the church. This honor is not randomly taken by the individual; it is God who calls. The church must guard against those who attempt to use the church for personal gain. The ordination process is one of the primary ways the church carries out this responsibility.

In conclusion, the organized church under the leadership of the Holy Spirit is charged with the responsibility of carrying out its responsibility of approving ministers who are called by the Lord. In His sovereign activity, God separates people for the work of ministry and calls them to their vocation. Those who minister must have a strong conviction that their calling is from God and cooperate with the church in its responsibility to recognize and affirm this call.

Questions

1. What is the origin of the word *clergy*?
2. What is the origin of the word *laity*?
3. List the differences between the role of the priest and prophet in the Old Testament.
4. How did priests come into their roles?
5. How did the prophets come into their roles?
6. How does the ministry of clergy and laity overlap?
7. Are there any ways the ministry of clergy and laity are separate? If so, how?
8. Do you believe all Christians are equally called to ministry? (Defend your answer.)
9. What is one of the primary responsibilities of the preacher?

Arndt, W., & Wilbur Gringrich, F. 1957. *A Greek-English Lexicon of the New Testament.* Chicago: The University of Chicago Press.

Colson, C. 1994. *Who Speaks for God?*. Chicago: Tyndale House Publishers.

Frank Viola, George Barna. 2008. *Pagan Christianity? Exploring the Roots of Our Church Practices.* Carol Stream: Tyndale House Publishers.

Guinness, O. 1998. *The Call.* Nashville, TN: Word Publisher.

Stevens, J. P. 1999. *The Other Six Days.* Grand Rapids MI : William B. Eerdsmans.

Stott, J. 2010. *The Radical Disciple.* Nottingham, England: InterVarsity Press.

Webster. 1996. *Webster's Encyclopedic Unabridged Dictionary of the English Language.* New York: Ramdom House Value Publishing, Inc.

10 *Has God Called You?*

"Have I not chosen you, the Twelve?"
—John 6:70 (NIV)

Has God Called You?

The special call to ministry is the highest honor a person can receive. When God calls, it is important to know that indeed it is the Lord who has called you and allow the assurance of that call to guide your career. The knowledge of that call is what sustains you during the challenging times in ministry.

The special calling can only rightly be understood in its relation to God's sovereign will and purpose. The Lord chooses whom He wills for His work. Christian ministers do not self-select into this calling. While they can resist God's call, it is not within their prerogative to initiate it. Only God does that, and He uses a variety of methods to communicate His calling to his servants.

Are All Called?

Jesus did not call everyone He met to leave their nets and follow Him. There was a select group of followers whom he called to leave their occupations and become His apprentices in ministry. He later designated them as apostles and emphasized to them, "Have I not chosen you, the Twelve?" (John 6:70 NIV). The apostles understood they had been specially called by Jesus to their ministry.

God's Providential Hand

It was seemingly a chance meeting with Jesus on the shores of Galilee that eternally changed the lives of these men. Four of them were fishing on Lake Galilee when a young rabbi from Nazareth invited them to leave their nets to follow Him. They could not possibly have imagined what lay ahead for them. That simple meeting and invitation proved to be pivotal in their careers.

No doubt, over time as they reflected on those first days with Jesus, they realized that encounter as a career-defining moment. There are times when an encounter seems to be very important at the moment but fades over time and is soon forgotten. But that was not the case for the disciples. That is why it is important to live each moment in the conscious presence of the Lord.

Sometimes the call of God begins with a simple impression. At the time, it only causes us to pause and give passing consideration to the idea. However, the thought keeps returning and over time begins to take root in our minds. As we mull it over, weighing its pros and cons, it grows from being just a plausible idea to a conviction about serving the Lord's work in a specific way.

Perhaps something similar happened to the disciples at the end of the story in chapter 9 of Matthew's Gospel. In that story, the crowd of people representing a wide range of human needs had come to Jesus seeking help.

Jesus took the opportunity to call His disciples' attention to their needs and compared these folks to a ripe harvest field. The disciples could see the brokenness of the people and were challenged to pray for workers to minister to these people.

At the time, the disciples were in the earlier phases of their apprenticeships and just beginning to comprehend the significance of Jesus's ministry. Likely, as they began to pray about the needs of the people, a sense of conviction began forming in their hearts and minds about what they could do to serve those needs. Over time, these ideas became convictions about how they could serve in the harvest fields of the world. Their callings were beginning to be shaped by their circumstances.

Recognizing the Lord's Voice

Sometimes the challenge for Christians is to distinguish between an impression that comes to us from time to time and the Lord's voice. Does a particular thought or idea come from the Lord, or is it just an impression that will go away with time? There are times when the call to ministry begins with an initial impression and over time grows to the point it becomes a conviction. To some extent, all sincere Christians will deal with this concern. How do we know the difference between the voice of Christ and an impression?

Jesus said, "My sheep hear my voice, and I know them, and they follow me" (John 10:27 KJV). But how do we know whether His voice is behind an impression when He is not physically present with us? Is this thought just a passing idea that will go away with time? Or is this the voice of the Lord speaking to me? If it is the Lord speaking, the idea will persist and over time become stronger.

Satan can impersonate an angel of enlightenment. The scriptures teach "Satan himself masquerades as an angel of light" (2 Corinthians 11:14 NIV). In other words, Satan can speak to us through impressions. However, he intends to mislead and confuse us about God's will. That is why the apostle John wrote to test the spirits. "Dear friends, do not believe every spirit, but test the spirits to see whether they are from God" (1 John 4:1 NIV). In other words, do not jump at every idea that comes to mind as being the voice of God. Rather, we should mull the idea over in our minds as we reflect on the scriptures and ask the Lord to make clear His will to us.

The Lord never leads us contrary to the scriptures. Our first question should be, "Is this impression in harmony with the Bible?" If it does not match the teaching of scripture, we can dismiss the idea as not coming from the Lord. The better acquainted we are with the scriptures, the better equipped we are to know whether an impression is scriptural.

The second question we should ask is, "What do other Christians think about the idea?" It is wise to seek the counsel of mature Christians. As members of the body of Christ, we have brothers and sisters who can help us sort through impressions. These spiritual counselors and mentors can help us avoid foolish and unwise decisions.

The third question we should ask about an impression is, "Does the idea bring a sense of peace from the Lord?" Impressions coming from the Lord are typically accompanied by an underlying peace, even when the risks are high. While we may have legitimate concerns about whether we can accomplish what the Lord is asking us to do, as we take steps forward in faith, we experience an increasing assurance about the future.

The fourth question we should ask is, "Does rejecting the idea seem to put distance between me and Christ?" Yielding to impressions coming from the Lord strengthen our relationship with Him. Ignoring or rejecting them causes us to experience a growing alienation from Him. Christ is very patient and will faithfully guide us along the paths of His calling if we are open to hearing His voice. If we have questions, we should ask Him to give us wisdom about the future. "If any of you lacks wisdom, you should ask God, who gives generously to all without finding fault, and it will be given to you" (James 1:5 NIV).

Confusion about the Call

Perhaps the greatest source of confusion about the call to ministry is spiritual apathy. Spiritual apathy happens when we fail to set aside the time, effort, and discipline required to maintain a vibrant relationship with Christ. We become careless about church attendance, rarely if ever read and study the scriptures, and fail to pray. Ignoring these practices causes

Christ to become distant in our lives and allows our spiritual fervor to cool. This often leads to confusion about our calling.

Our relationship with Christ is like any other relationship in life. As we spend time with friends, engage in the activities they enjoy, and fellowship with them, those friendships flourish. If we fail to spend time with our friends, stop doing the things they enjoy, and seek to live our lives apart from them, those friendships languish.

The same is true of our relationship with Christ. As we engage in those activities that draw us deeper into our relationship with Him, it flourishes. On the other hand, if we fail to spend time with Christ, disregard His teachings, and seek to live our lives apart from Him and His influence, our relationship with Him languishes. This affects our ability to hear His voice, especially the call to ministry.

Confusion about the call to ministry also arises when we are unwilling to surrender our lives to His lordship. We hold back, not allowing God to lead us in the direction of His calling. We resist both His lordship and the idea of ministry. Instead, we choose to pursue personal goals, attempting to dismiss the idea of ministry. Inevitably, that puts distance between us and Christ and brings spiritual confusion.

It is unwise to set conditions on how far we are willing to allow the Lord to lead us in ministry. Answering the special call involves submission to His lordship and a willingness to take risks for Him. While it is easier to retreat to what is familiar and safe rather than step out by faith into the unknown, it is wiser to take that risk in the long run. Jesus said, "For whoever wants to save their life will lose it, but whoever loses their life for me will save it" (Luke 9:24 NIV).

Jesus invited the rich young ruler to become His disciple. Instead, he rejected Christ's lordship and chose to follow self-serving purposes—he refused Jesus's call to sell his possession, give the proceeds to the poor, and take up his cross to follow Him. He turned his back on ministry because of the price he was asked to pay. Only Jesus fully understands our potential under His lordship.

The higher path in life is always the pathway of faith, following Christ, trusting Him with our future, and surrendering our lives to His lordship. There are great eternal values that await people of great faith. The giants of faith make their relationship with the Lord a priority in their lives and allow their faith to shape the trajectory of their careers.

A friend who entered the ministry in his late twenties and has served several years as a lead pastor shared his story. When he finished high school, he had questions about whether he should go into the ministry. In the end, he decided that the ministry required too much sacrifice and chose to pursue other goals, attempting to dismiss the idea of becoming a minister.

As he pursued these goals, he drifted away from Christ. However, instead of finding fulfillment and satisfaction, his life began to fill with disappointment and confusion. It was not long before he recognized his life was spiraling downward and toward being out of control. Eventually, he came to realize that his career choices were destroying his life. After a couple of poor decisions, he turned to the Lord for help. When he began to seek the Lord in earnest, the idea of ministry once again returned to his thoughts.

As his faith grew, so did the idea of ministry. He soon came to a crossroads—was he going to answer the call to ministry or continue pursuing other career goals? Was he willing to step out in faith and trust Christ with his future? When he took the initial steps by enrolling in a ministry-training program, his faith grew stronger and the peace he once knew returned. Each step of faith he took toward ministry caused his sense of calling to grow stronger.

Overcoming Obstacles

A growing number of young people preparing to enter the ministry are drawn toward choosing dual majors in college. The number of churches that can support a full-time minister is declining. These young folks recognize that God is calling them to ministry, and they want to be able to financially support a family. They are not necessarily choosing to resist the Lord's call.

Jesus said to his disciples, "My yoke is easy and my burden light" (Matthew 11:30 NIV). While He expects His followers to be sold out in their devotion to His cause, He does not place unreasonable demands on them. He is the Good Shepherd who provides protection and pasture for His children.

Enduring Hard Places in Ministry

There are times when the ministry brings times of testing and trial. Ministry is often listed as being among the most difficult jobs in America. A recent statistic indicates that many ministers will leave the ministry within the next few years. Further, only a growing percentage of current ministers expect to retire from ministry at the end of their careers. They anticipate switching to another career before they retire. However, difficult situations should not cause us to abandon ministry.

The Lord is not a hard taskmaster who demands the impossible by laying heavy burdens on us just to see us suffer. While the call to ministry requires a strong faith and at times may challenge us, the Lord always gives us enough grace to do His work. Paul had a physical challenge that seemed to limit his ability to minister—a thorn in his flesh. On several occasions, he sought the Lord for healing from this problem. God's answer to Paul was not to heal him but to assure him that he would give him the necessary grace to minister even within those weaknesses. (See 2 Corinthians 12:7–9.)

In an earlier story, Brother Andrew shared that when he went to Bible school, the physical problems with his back were so severe that he could not expect to be approved by a mission board for missionary work. Yet events and circumstances continued to cross his pathway that affirmed his calling. As he faithfully took each step of faith in the direction of his calling, doors of opportunity providentially continued to open for him. In the early days of his career, he overcame seemingly impossible circumstances to do missionary work.

During this time, while struggling with severe back pain, he transported Bibles to Christians behind the Iron Curtain. Those doors of ministry continued to open for him. The healing of his back came later because of a plane crash. At that point, his ministry had grown to the point where he was doing a lot of international travel for fundraising. On one of those trips, he was injured in a plane crash. At first, the injury appeared to further exacerbate the problems with his back. However, he discovered that because of the accident, his back began to heal.

At times, the Lord calls us to serve under difficult circumstances. The Lord called Jeremiah to be His faithful voice to the people of Judah and Jerusalem during their final days before Babylon's overthrow. That was a tough assignment. At one point, Jeremiah faced such intense opposition and persecution that he decided to leave the ministry—he would remain silent and no longer preach. His preaching was only bringing him more persecution, rejection, and hardship.

However, when he grew silent, the Lord's words became like "a fire shut up in my bones in his bones" (Jeremiah 20:9 NIV), and he grew weary attempting to hold it in. What he discovered was that God's grace sustains His servants and enables them to remain faithful even in the tough times of ministry.

Daniel found himself in an unimaginable situation—being a captive in a foreign land. In addition to not knowing where he would live next, to survive he had to learn their language and culture. However, in spite of the circumstances of life, he had a strong trust that God would sustain him. Early on, he requested to be exempted from eating the meat that was devoted to the king's idols. As a result, he and his Hebrew brothers grew healthier, and their faith grew stronger. In the end, Daniel served in the cabinet as special counsel to several kings of two nations.

Nehemiah was born in a foreign land and grew up wondering what living in his homeland would be like. When he found himself in a strategic place of influence, he used his situation to serve the Lord's work. When he heard about the pathetic condition in his homeland, he realized that if given the opportunity, he could make a difference. His knowledge about administration and finance compelled him to make a difference in his homeland. He began praying about the situation and walking through the doors that were providentially opening for him. In the end, he was able to rebuild Jerusalem's walls within fifty-two days and restore the infrastructure of Jerusalem. As governor of the region working with Ezra, he educated the people about God's laws.

Paul questioned whether his past life of persecuting the church disqualified him from being a minister of the gospel. Yet the Lord knew all about his past when he called him to be an apostle to the Gentiles.

God turned his weakness into a strength for Paul. Because of his past of persecuting the church, Paul was not deterred when faced with fierce opposition and persecution. He knew what it was like to be on the other side of the fight. The Lord used those experiences to enable Paul to preach the gospel in those areas of the world that were hostile to the gospel message.

God used the circumstances and experiences of Jeremiah, Nehemiah, Daniel, and Paul to shape their callings and enable them to minister effectively. God can use all the circumstances of our lives, including our poor choices and the tragedies of life, to prepare us for the work that He calls us to do.

Is the Call Ever Rescinded?

A question that sometimes arises when the special call to ministry is discussed is, "Does the Lord ever rescind the call to ministry?" Practically all denominations ordain people for life.

There are times when the circumstances of life make it impractical or impossible to continue in ministry or, if the person is not already in the ministry, to enter the ministry. These circumstances include illnesses, accidents, and financial obligations that were created by our poor choices or that were imposed on us. The scriptures teach that we are to act responsibly concerning our other obligations in life. They too are a part of our calling in life.

Some become distracted by other goals and leave the ministry—often in the quest for money. Others simply withdraw from ministry because of discouragement or feeling they are a failure in ministry. Others have questioned if they misunderstood their calling.

Ministers do not leave the ministry because there is an overabundance of workers for the harvest. The need for workers has continued unabated from the time of Christ right up to the present. The call for workers is a need that never goes away.

The question is raised, "Does the Lord ever release a person from their call?" Some answer yes, while others answer no. Those who answer no point that "God's gifts and his call are irrevocable" (Romans 11:29 NIV).

Those who answer yes point to Judas in the New Testament, Saul in the Old Testament, and others who were unfaithful to their calling.

The truth lies between to two. In practically every situation, those who leave the ministry never completely lose the desire to serve in ministry. It may become dulled to the point there is very little stirring, but it never goes away completely. There are circumstances when continuing in ministry is impractical or impossible. In some instances, the person may discover new and creative ways of ministering under the altered circumstances in their lives. In other situations, they may live with emptiness in their lives.

The gifts and talents given to the person at birth that naturally equip them for ministry are not typically taken away. Those gifts can be developed to higher levels that enable them to minister more effectively, or they can be laid aside and become dull and ineffective. Those natural talents generally remain with the person throughout their lifetime. However, sometimes they may be altered or lost through tragedies, accidents, and illnesses. Though, in most cases, the talents that equip a person for the Lord's work are not taken away. They remain an integral part of the person's life, beckoning them to use their talents in the Lord's work.

But there is a part that may be lost—the Lord's anointing. It is the Spirit's anointing that elevates a person's gifts and abilities to another level of effectiveness. A good example of this is Peter's preaching on the Day of Pentecost. On that occasion, three thousand people were convinced about the truth of Peter's message and turned to Christ for salvation. A well-known evangelist lecturing a group of seminary students stated that is what separates preaching from speaking. He concluded that preaching cannot take place without the anointing of God's Spirit. I agree with him. A speech may be powerful and persuasive, but it is not preaching unless it is anointed by the Spirit. When that occurs, it is preaching.

God's anointing may be forfeited through disobedience and rebellion. When people turn their backs on God and reject His lordship, the Spirit is grieved, and His anointing may be lost, reducing them to a level where they are no longer capable of leading God's work. That was the case of both Judas and King Saul. Judas was called by Jesus to be one of His apostles. However, he turned his back on his calling and betrayed Jesus. Because of his love for money, he sold his soul for thirty pieces of silver.

Betraying Jesus left him in a desperate condition, and in his despair, he took his own life.

After King Saul was anointed by Samuel to lead Israel as their king, he discovered the Lord's anointing equipped him to lead the nation. When the men of Jabesh Gilead came to him asking for help after Nahash the Ammonite told them that he was going to gouge out all their right eyes if they did not submit to his demands, the Spirit of the Lord came upon Saul, and he assembled the Israelites. The situation filled him with righteous indignation and with the Lord's anointing. With the Lord's anointing, he formed an army and soundly defeated Nahash and the Ammonites. (See 1 Samuel 10:1–11.)

However, years later after he had repeatedly disobeyed the Lord's commands, Saul discovered the Lord's anointing had left him. In the heat of the battle with the Philistines, when he urgently needed direction from the Lord, he discovered that he was now alienated from God. In desperation, he turned to a witch for guidance and told her, "God has departed from me and he no longer answers me" (1 Samuel 28:15 NIV). In that desperate hour, Saul took his own life. Both Judas and Saul were specially called by God and anointed for their work. However, both turned their backs on God and ended up committing suicide because of their desperate situations.

The Heavy Lifting Is Done by the Lord

Ministers quickly discover that success in the Lord's work does not primarily come because of human skill and ingenuity. A minister cannot bring a single person from spiritual death to spiritual life. Only God can do that. Thus, in the most basic sense, it is the Lord who builds the house. He often intervenes in unexpected ways to accomplish His purposes. These events cannot be predicted and, in the end, often are miracles more than anything else that lead to some of the greatest successes in ministry.

At the same time, the ministers must realize that they must be wise servants as they lead the Lord's work. Ignoring sound practices often leads to disastrous results. In his letter to the Corinthian Christians, Paul described his work among them as being that of a wise builder and described his job to serve the Lord's work as a good steward. However, in the end, it was up to God to give the increase. (See 1 Corinthians 3:5–15.)

Faithful Service Advances the Lord's Kingdom

Another factor that underlies success in ministry is faithfulness. There is no substitute for this character quality. Paul describes it as being a fruit of the Spirit. In the parable of the stewards, Jesus taught that those who are faithful with small responsibilities are also the ones who are faithful in the larger ones. Those who are faithful in the small areas of life can anticipate being entrusted with increasing responsibilities. (See Matthew 25:14–30.)

God knows the future in ways that we cannot imagine. He is the God of eternity who created time and is beyond it. Because of his foreknowledge, God has a way of providentially ordering the circumstance and events of our lives to accomplish His purpose in ways that are beyond our ability to understand or even imagine. He knows how to cause us to be in the right location under specific circumstances at a particular time for His purposes, while all the time it is hidden from us.

My first ministry assignment was a church plant. On our first day in town, we thought we had an apartment that was ready for us to move into. However, it did not work out, and the next morning, our furniture was scheduled to arrive. We were desperately praying and searching for an available apartment. At breakfast the next morning, we were frantically searching the local newspaper for an apartment and spotted an ad for what appeared to be a suitable apartment. We hurried across the street to the landlord's place of business to inquire about the apartment.

We were surprised when the owner handed us the keys and told us to look at the apartment and let him know if we wanted it. We found that it was suitable for our purposes and immediately returned to sign the lease, without knowing the location of the apartment in reference to the building that had been leased for the church plant. After signing the lease, we hurried over to meet the movers and led them to our new home. Later that evening, we were surprised to discover that our apartment was less than a block away from the building that had been leased for the church plant. It turned out to be one of the nicest apartments we have ever lived in. But that was not all that God had in mind for us that day.

A few weeks later, the man who lived next door came over to introduce himself. Over time, our friendship with him grew. He contributed to the remodeling work we were doing on the building and from time to time would give financially to the church. Periodically, he and his wife would attend our church. That relationship continued to grow over the years, even after we had moved on to another ministry.

One day while I was serving in my first job as dean of a college, he called and invited me to come and visit him. While we were visiting with him, he informed me that he had known about the college for years and was delighted I was working there. He also let me know that he planned to give a gift to the college in part because I was working there, and he knew me. It turned out that his gift was one of the largest gifts the college had ever received in its eighty-five-year history.

We could not imagine all of that happening that morning at breakfast when we were frantically searching for an apartment. But God did, and behind the scenes, He was providentially orchestrating the events of that day. (My sister-in-law believes it was God's providential hand because it was through our ministry in that city she met her husband.) The more we invite Christ to become a part of our decisions, the easier it becomes to align our lives and careers with His plans for us.

New Types of Ministries in the Future

What will ministry look like in the next few decades? It is hard to imagine the new types of ministries that will emerge over the next three or four decades. Our world is rapidly changing. The needs of the people around us are changing. With these changes taking place, the contours of ministry will change. One hundred years ago, it would have been impossible to imagine the church world as it exists today.

When I drive through the Midwest countryside, I see many white-frame churches dotting the landscape of the countryside that are a testimony to what ministry looked like several decades ago. Although many of these country churches continue to exist, most of them no longer have the same amount of influence in the communities they once held. A few generations ago, they were spiritual hubs in many farming communities. Today, as society has changed and the needs of people have changed, these houses of worship have also changed.

Many parachurch ministries have emerged over the past fifty years to support the church as it seeks to accomplish its mission. No doubt many more will emerge over the next few decades as new needs arise. Even though it is humanly impossible to see all the new types of ministries that will emerge, the Lord sees those needs and is at work preparing His servants to lead those ministries. He is planting seed ideas in the minds of young Christians about how to serve these needs.

A few years ago, I attempted to outline what I thought the shape the church would look like over the next few decades. My goal was to develop a profile of the church that would inform ministry-training programs about preparing students for ministries of the future. What I quickly discovered was that even by accessing the best research, predictions regarding the future of ministry are fraught with many errors. While we may be able to get a few things right with our models, we will miss some very strategic elements about the future. Changes will take place that no one could have foreseen. However, the Lord knows about these changes and is at work preparing His servants for the future.

When Paul encountered Jesus on his way to Damascus, he could not imagine all the Lord had in mind for his future. Following that experience, he spent time reflecting on what had just happened to him and perhaps thinking about how to evangelize his hometown. A little later, Barnabas traveled to Tarsus to find him and introduced him to the Antioch and Jerusalem churches.

Sometime later, the Spirit called them to go west to evangelize the Gentiles first in Cyprus and then in Asia Minor. They could not possibly have known that, within a generation, Jerusalem would be gone and the center of Christianity would be shifting away from Jerusalem and moving in the direction of Alexandra and Rome. Reading about their story in Acts, one gets the impression that each day was a step of faith. They were unsure of how things were going to turn out and just kept going forward by faith.

When they landed on the coast of Asia Minor, John Mark, Barnabas's nephew, left them and returned home. Because Mark left them when they entered Asia Minor, later when they prepared to revisit those new churches, Paul refused to allow Mark to go with them. As a result, Paul took Silas and traveled the interior roads to revisit the churches in Asia Minor, while Barnabas took Mark and revisited the churches in Cyprus. At that time, no one could have imagined that young Mark would someday write the Gospel that bears his name. But God did!

On his second missionary journey with Silas, Paul could not have known that he would induct Timothy into the ministry at Lystra. Neither could he have known that he would meet up with Luke at Troas. But God did! He could not have known that Luke would later compile his Gospel and the history of the early church in the book of Acts. But God did! God sees the future in ways that we cannot comprehend.

The same is true for us today. The Lord knows the changes that will take place tomorrow. Even now, He is at work preparing the hearts of those whom He will call into ministry for a future that is not known today. Our job is to take steps of faith in the direction of the Lord's call.

God's Providential Guidance Is Best Understood by Looking Back

Because it is beyond our ability to know the future, we must go forward in faith. God's providence is best understood by recalling His faithfulness in the past—by recalling His faithfulness in earlier times. When we do this, we find new courage to trust Him for the future. One of the ways to do this is a prayer journal. It allows us to go back, read our prayers, and recall the Lord's faithfulness to us in the difficult times of life.

While there are times when the Lord gives us glimpses of the future, those visions are limited in scope and not fleshed out. The Lord has many surprises for us as we follow His call.

When Bill and Vonette Bright founded CRU, they could not have imagined that it would grow to have a worldwide influence. But God did! When Billy Graham held his first tent meeting in Los Angles, he could not have imagined how this ministry would grow into the Billy Graham Evangelistic organization. But God did! Today, there are new types of ministries that are only in their embryo stages in the minds and hearts of the Lord's servants. We must learn to obediently follow the Lord and trust Him to guide us into the future.

Ultimately, the Value of Our Ministry Is for the Lord to Measure

Ultimately, we must realize that we may never know the significance of our ministry this side of eternity. It is impossible for us to fully evaluate the success of a ministry. Jesus cautions us that there are "many who are first will be last, and the last first" (Mark 10:31 NIV). In other words, only the Master can truly evaluate the degree of success of His servants.

Just because our ministry never rises to regional, national, or international significance does not mean it is insignificant to God. When Mark was compiling his Gospel, he could not have imagined that his work would be read by millions of believers over two millennia and be embraced by Christian as a part of their canon of scriptures. But God did!

Layton Ford tells about Ruth Graham returning to China to visit the area where she grew up as a child. Her father had served as a medical missionary in that area before he was forced to flee because of the Communist takeover. The work had originally been pioneered by a missionary who spent twenty-five years winning twenty-three converts. During that time, he would sometimes return home having stones thrown at him and being spit upon. Ruth Graham's father had followed him as a missionary doctor but within a few years was forced to leave because of the political situation.

After the Communist takeover and thirty years of oppression, she wanted to know if any Christians survived the persecution. Eventually, she was able to visit her childhood home—the same area where that pioneer missionary who first took the gospel to the area had labored twenty-five years to win twenty-three converts. When she inquired if there were any Christians left after Communist oppression and persecution, what she learned astounded her. They estimated 140,000 Christians were living in that area. That pioneer missionary's faithful service had planted seeds that produced a harvest beyond his wildest imagination. Rather than destroying the church, persecution had only caused it to flourish (Ford, 1991).

With only a few Bibles, while enduring severe persecution, where did those Chinese Christians get the strength to persist in their faith? No doubt the examples of that pioneer missionary and Ruth Graham's parents had embodied the model of a living Christ and a faith that was anchored in Christ. They had witnessed Christianity lived out under difficult circumstances.

If that pioneer missionary could have seen how his labors in Christ would produce such a harvest, he would have found great courage for his ministry. Yet during his lifetime, it was hidden from him. He could only go forward by faith, entrusting the results to the Lord. Only faith can sustain that kind of ministry.

The Future Is Unknown

In this journey of life, we never know what lies around the corner in our lives or careers. There can be setbacks. Instead of going forward, sometimes things seem to be going in reverse. This can leave us to question what the Lord has in mind for us. Does this mean we should give up and leave the ministry, or should we seek to persist in the ministry? The Lord is a faithful guide in this journey of life and will be faithful to guide us in the paths of His calling.

Questions

1. Do you believe the Lord has called you to the ministry? (If so, describe that call.)
2. How were the disciples Peter, James, John, and Andrew called into the ministry? (Read their stories in Matthew 4:18–22; Mark 1:16–20; Luke 5:2–11; and John 1:35–42.)
3. List the basic questions to ask regarding whether an impression is from the Lord.
4. How does our relationship with Christ affect our understanding of the call to ministry?

5. Describe your present relationship with Christ.
6. Do you believe the call to ministry is ever rescinded? (Defend your answer.)
7. Identify a current need in the church that is not presently being served. Are you willing to pray for the Lord to send someone to serve that need?
8. How has God been faithful to answer your prayers in the past?

Ford, Leighton. 1991. *Transforming Leadership Jesus' Way of Creating Vision, Shaping Values & Empowering Change*. Downers Grove, IL: InterVarsity Press.

Bibliography

Arndt, W., & Wilbur Gringrich, F. 1957. *A Greek-English Lexicon of the New Testament*. Chicago: The University of Chicago Press.

Ballard, J., & Currier, S. 2005. *I Belong Here*. Memphis, TN: The Master Design.

Barna, F. V. 2002. *Pagan Christianity*. Carol Stream: Tyndale House/BarnaBooks.

Becker, V. 1996. *The Calling*. Moorings: Nashville.

Bill T. Arnold, Bryan E. Beyer . 1998. *Encountering the Old Testament*. Grand Rapids, MI: Baker Book House.

Bolles, R. 1999. *What Color Is your Parachute*. Berkley CA: Ten Speed Press.

Bookless, D. 2008. *Planet Wise*. Downers Grove: IVP.

Bright, B. 1995. *The Coming Revival*. Orlando: New Life Publications.

Bright, B. 2003. *The Journey Home*. Nashville: Thomas Nelson Publishers.

Bright, B. (2009). *Seven Basic Steps to Successful Fasting and Prayer*. Peachtree, GA: Campus Crusade for Christ.

Buechner, F. 1973. *Wishful Thinking: The Seeker's ABCs*. New York: Harper.

Colson, C. 1994. *Who Speaks for God?*. Chicago: Tyndale House Publishers.

Dallas Willard. 2010. *A Place for Truth*. Downers Grove, IL: InterVarsity Press.

Ford, L. 1991. *Transforming Leadership Jesus' Way of Creating Vision, Shaping Values & Empowering Change*. Downers Grove, IL: InterVarsity Press.

Frank Viola, George Barna. 2008. *Pagan Christianity? Exploring the Roots of Our Church Practices*. Carol Stream: Tyndale House Publishers.

Graham, B. 1984. *Peace With God*. Waco: Word Books.

Guinness, O. 2001. *Doing Well and Doing Good*. Colorado Springs, Colorado: NavPress.

Guinness, O. 1998. *The Call*. Nashville, TN: Word Publisher.

Keener, C. S. 1993. *The IVP Bible background Commentary*. Downers Grove: IVP.

M. Robert Mullholland, J. 2001. *Shaped by the Word: The Power of Scripture in Spiritual Formation,*. Nashville: Upper Room Books.

Moore, R. 2010. *Christianity Today*, p. 20.

Mulholland, M. R. 2001. *Shaped by the Word:The Poert of Scripture in Spiritual Formation*. Word Press.

Mullahand, R. (n.d.).

Pascal, B. 2007, September 14. *the heartshaped vacuum that can only be filled by god*. Retrieved December 4, 2012, from Vineyard Muses: http://takmeng.blogspot.com/

Richard Taylor. 1983. *Beacon Dictionary of Theology*. Kansas City: Beacon Hill Press of Kansas.

Richardson, M. 2000. *Amazing Faith*. Colorado Springs: WaterBrook Press.

Schmidt, A. J. 2004. *How Christiniaty Changed The World*. Grand Rapids: Zondervan.

Smith, M. B. 1991. *Knowing God's Will*. Downers Grove, IL: InterVarsity Press.

Stevens, J. P. 1999. *The Other Six Days*. Grand Rapids MI : William B. Eerdsmans.

Stott, J. 1996. *Guard the Truth*. Dowers Grove: Inter-Varsity Press.

Stott, J. 2010. *The Radical Disciple*. Nottingham, England: InterVarsity Press.

VanGemeren, W. A. 1997. *New International Dictionary of Old Testament Theology and Exegesis, Vol. 3*. Grand Rapids, : Zondervan.

Walton, J., Matthews, V., & Chavalas, M. 2000. *The IVP Bible Background Commentary Old Testament*. Downers Grove, IL: InteVarsity Press.

Webster. 1996. *Webster's Encyclopedic Unabridged Dictionary of the English Language*. New York: Ramdom House Value Publishing, Inc.

Wright, N. T. 2008. *Surprised by Hope: Rethinking Heaven, the Resurrection, and the Mission of the Church*. New York, NY: Harper Collins.

Printed in the United States
by Baker & Taylor Publisher Services